Captain Otway Burns

Captain Otway Burns

Tar Heel Privateer, Legislator and Naval Hero of the War of 1812

Michael K. Brantley

McFarland & Company, Inc., Publishers
Jefferson, North Carolina

ISBN (print) 978-1-4766-9712-3
ISBN (ebook) 978-1-4766-5748-6

LIBRARY OF CONGRESS CATALOGING DATA ARE AVAILABLE

Library of Congress Control Number 2026002659

© 2026 Michael K. Brantley. All rights reserved

No part of this book may be reproduced or transmitted in any form or by any means, electronic or mechanical, including photocopying or recording, or by any information storage and retrieval system, without permission in writing from the publisher.

Front cover image: oil painting of Otway Burns by F. Mahler, created between 1875 and 1895 (courtesy of the North Carolina Department of Natural and Cultural Resources).

Printed in the United States of America

*McFarland & Company, Inc., Publishers
Box 611, Jefferson, North Carolina 28640
www.mcfarlandpub.com*

In memory of
Penny Daly, Beverly Cooper,
Bonnie Kane, and Ed Holloway—
teachers who put me on a path
of reading, writing, and research
that changed my life

Acknowledgments

A book doesn't happen without a lot of help, and most of the time those who provide it like to stay in the background. They should get a moment. Early on, I greatly benefited from spending some time with a few of the Fish House Liars, particularly Durward "Dee" Lewis and Rodney Kemp from Carteret County, North Carolina. They helped me make the most of the resources at the History Museum of Carteret County in Morehead City, North Carolina. Also helpful in that first couple of years were the folks at the State Archives of North Carolina in Raleigh. Amelia Dees-Killette of the Swansboro Historical Association gave me wonderful access to files and records at the Swansboro Area Heritage Center, which filled in so many gaps late in the process. The North Caroliniana Society provided a grant so many years ago to get me started that they may wonder what happened to me or to the project. They helped me acquire and access some tremendous resources. Of course, I am grateful beyond words to everyone at McFarland for believing in this project and agreeing that this story needed to be out in the world. It's a feeling hard to describe for a writer. And finally, my first reader and close adviser on all my work, my favorite historian and my wife, Kristi Brantley, provided support from the beginning through all the dead ends and big discoveries; I've lost count of the revisions.

Table of Contents

Acknowledgments   vi

Preface   1

1. A Lawyer in the Neuse River   7
2. Early Life on the Water   15
3. War Comes with Britain   24
4. Privateering   34
5. The First Tour of the *Snap Dragon*   45
6. The War Hits Hard   64
7. The Second Tour of the *Snap Dragon*   70
8. Dustups and Adventures Between Voyages   85
9. The Third Tour of the *Snap Dragon*   89
10. The War Ends   97
11. Postwar Ventures   105
12. The Legislator   124
13. Hard Times   136
14. Legacy of Legends and Lies   141

Epilogue   159

Nautical and Shipping Terms   175

Table of Contents

Chapter Notes   179
Bibliography   187
Index   191

Preface

I'D SEEN THE WHITE-LETTERED "OTWAY" on the green state highway sign on the drive from Beaufort to Harker's Island, North Carolina, a time or two, but I didn't really know the name. Then one night on vacation, my family was eating in a since-closed Swansboro seafood restaurant in the next county over and there was the story of Otway Burns right there on my paper placemat. It wasn't really the story, just a brief sketch of a ship's captain from the War of 1812. It was interesting enough that I scribbled a couple of items in a notebook. That was probably close to 25 years ago. More than a decade later, I ran across a story about this same man and it ended with him throwing a lawyer who had insulted him into the Neuse River. This was a character I needed to know more about.

It wasn't easy finding things about Otway Burns. I attended North Carolina public schools, took a mandatory class called North Carolina History, earned a history minor (almost a major) in college and took another North Carolina history course in college and never once heard the name. Yet this man was the state's first naval hero, cast the deciding vote on several pieces of key state legislation in the early 19th century, supplied bricks for a fort that is still standing nearly 200 years later, has two towns named after him, and has a boatload of adventures and stories as his legacy.

Otway Burns was a merchant sea captain, a patriot, a privateer and war hero, a productive and independent legislator, a successful business executive and entrepreneur, an unsuccessful debt collector, a shipbuilder, and a good friend and community supporter to those

Preface

who knew him. He also had a short temper; was stubborn, brave, and headstrong; had a distinct sense of right and wrong that didn't always sit well with others; and could be a formidable and physical enemy.

He was married three times, with the first marriage ending in a tumultuous separation and eventual custody battle; was turned out of politics because he was too independent as a politician; and despite becoming a wealthy, self-made man, spent his last years destitute after falling into financial ruin and obscurity.

Burns displayed an "iron will, courage, endurance, self-confidence, a direct manner, a forceful personality, a decisive and creative leadership style, mastery of seamanship, and colorful character."[1] Although accurate, that description doesn't even begin to tell his story.

Burns was also one of the few heroes of the War of 1812, America's first "forgotten war," it seems, a title most often ascribed to the Korean War in the mid–20th century. It's now more than 200 years in the past and it still isn't covered heavily in schools—the British burning of Washington, D.C., and the Battle of New Orleans might be the extent of what is mentioned. Part of that is because of the strange conduct and causes of the war; there was no real moral issue at stake for the young nation—it was mostly a fledgling country trying to earn some respect and protection from bullies on the high seas. The British, of course, saw the war quite differently. They saw themselves engaged in a fight to the death with Napoleonic France and viewed their American cousins as very nonchalant and apathetic trading partners who failed to see the global complications of European conquest—an irony, for sure.

The life of Otway Burns seems like an action movie at times, with adventures on the high seas that could easily be a big screen hit. There's melodrama and political intrigue and betrayal, a downward spiral of a former celebrity, and the repair of that legacy half a century later.

Burns was a notable character in North Carolina, the United States, and maritime history but someone whose story has been

Preface

relegated to the dusty attic of remembrance. This book offers his adventure and the telling of a conflict that could more accurately be called the Second War for Independence.

It's also about how a small group of lawmakers tried to drag North Carolina out of its Rip Van Winkle state and into a more modern and competitive present. Politics has always been brutal, perhaps overly so to the altruistic. It's about how trusting the wrong people can lead to ruinous downfalls.

This period in America's history deserves more attention, as does this remarkable character who, even though memorialized in some notable ways, is largely forgotten not only in the United States but even in his home state. His story deserves to be told not only because he was a war hero but also because of the lasting impact he had on his country and his state. He is a great example of fleeting fame and a fickle public.

As with many larger-than-life characters, there are plenty of myths and legends surrounding Otway Burns. This book sorts them out in an informative and entertaining way, even though differentiating fact from fiction may be difficult at times—one often seems like the other. Many of the true stories seem more outlandish than the made-up ones.

This book covers Burns and the area around him because of how it shaped him. There is a sketch of the War of 1812 that is far from comprehensive but gives a basic outline of a war that is perhaps only challenged by the Spanish-American War as the conflict typical Americans know the least about but put the United States on the footing that would lead to tremendous expansion in the 19th century. What was happening in North Carolina during this war is key to understanding why privateers were desperately needed and the impact they had.

Research for this book was about as nonlinear as it gets. Often in trying to verify stories, I spent time in museums, libraries, and various archives and countless more hours scouring online records and old newspapers, many of which were incomplete. At times, it

Preface

may seem to heavily lean on the *North Carolina University Magazine* from the mid–1850s and a couple of works about privateers; this is because the ship's logs were lost long ago and those volumes offered what amounted to transcriptions of the records. There are not a lot of books out there on Otway Burns: there is *Captain Otway Burns: Patriot, Privateer, and Legislator* by the man's grandson, who was trying to rehab the old captain's image in the early 1900s, and Ruth Barbour's novel, *Cruise of the* Snap Dragon, which is a read primarily for entertainment. This book is really the only one that pulls the war years, political career, business ventures, personal dramas, misadventures, and myths all together in one work. Finally, it is hard to ignore the irony of how history has treated two of the more notable sailors on the Atlantic coast in the 18th and 19th centuries. There is the notorious Edward Teach (or Thatch among several recorded spellings), also known as Blackbeard, who proudly laid claim to the title of pirate and lived a brutally criminal life committing robbery, murder, bribery, and a host of other major crimes. Then there is Otway Burns, a man of principle, a patriot who fought for his country, and a public servant who insisted on doing what he believed was right, even when it cost him personally. It enraged Burns whenever he was referred to as a pirate, as he never acted without full licensure of the United States government.

More than 200 years later, the public seems intrigued by pirates, with festivals in many towns celebrating the legacy of those who terrorized the high seas. *Black Sails* was a popular and Emmy-winning historical fiction television series from 2014 to 2017 that brought many famous and lesser-known pirates to the public eye in a humanizing way. There are coffee shops and restaurants and many other ventures sporting the name Blackbeard, as well as apparel featuring his flag and image.

On the other hand, Burns was a naval hero, a champion of the people, and a man who lived like a real-life action hero—but he is mostly remembered only by those local historians who tell his story

Preface

at community gatherings, the citizens of his two namesake townships, and curious tourists who stop to see one of his statues and are left to wonder why they hadn't heard of him before.

1

A Lawyer in the Neuse River

There may be some variation in the telling, but one thing is for sure: on a warm September day in 1812, Otway Burns tossed a New Bern, North Carolina, attorney into the chilly waters of the Neuse River. The man, Francis Martin, had big aspirations for his public image and an eye toward elected office and was trying to make a name for himself by rallying the citizenry around a common cause: get the privateers supplying and filling crews out of the port town.

New Bern, North Carolina, was buzzing with activity. The city, which had been the state capital before the American Revolution, is seated between the Neuse and Trent Rivers, which run to the Atlantic Ocean. The town was far enough into the interior for ships to safely refit, repair, and supply before heading back into the ocean. A second war with Britain was newly underway and the activity in town bordered on chaos. All the reasons that ships were docked put the locals at risk to attack or even invasion from the most powerful navy in the world. North Carolina, like most of the country's coastline, was woefully undefended and unprepared for war.

Martin was at the docks, taking his turn on the stump, trying to wind up the citizenry to get the ruffians out of New Bern and not give the British an easy target. He likely had a speaking horn to project not only to the crowd but also to seem bold by sending it out toward the anchored ships where these men watched from a distance. After railing about privateers in general, he loudly called Burns a "licensed robber." It's not noted whether he saw a rowboat quickly moving across the river, the crew straining to rapidly bring a man in the full naval dress of a captain to shore.

Although only of average size, the captain's weathered face was scarlet with a fury that powered his sinewy body shaped by nearly two decades of the hard life that was seafaring at the turn of the 19th century. He went straight for Martin and not one person stepped forward to get in his way. His temper was known and another recent episode he'd been at the center of was still the talk of the town. No one wanted to be in the way of Captain Otway Burns when he was in this state.

In one quick motion, the enraged Burns lifted the lawyer by the back of his collar and the seat of his pants and threw him into the chilly, brackish waters of the Neuse River. Burns stood on the dock and watched the lawyer try to tread water in his suit, regain his wits, and make a decision about what course of action might be wise. Burns refused to allow anyone to help Martin or to let him regain dry ground out of the water until he apologized for basically calling the captain a pirate. Martin realized he had no choice and no chance of salvaging his pride. The apology came. The sea captain turned, anger still simmering, and stepped off the pier and back on the longboat where the crewmen put their backs into getting him back to their ship.

Burns had just answered a personal insult with what he considered necessary but not excessive violence. He'd done it in front of witnesses, damn any consequences that may result, something he'd done for years and that would drive him for the coming decades. Many times, this force-of-nature attitude would steel and serve the captain well, and other times it would prove to be his undoing.

This episode was one of the first recorded notorious scenes in the Otway Burns story, a man whose life was a series of tall tales and truths that were so intertwined that they are often difficult to separate. It's part of what makes him such an interesting character whose actions and contributions should not be forgotten, even if his story seems like a Greek tragedy at times.

1. A Lawyer in the Neuse River

For example, there are several variations to this particular story. A magazine article in 1941 says that Burns snatched Martin off the street after being rowed ashore by his men.[1] Another magazine account in 1855 says that Martin yelled his insults from the docks out to Burns' ship and that Burns rowed to shore immediately.[2] Some early accounts of the episode even wrongly identify the attorney as Francis Xavier Martin, who was a litigator and powerful political figure in New Bern, served in the state legislature, and owned a local newspaper. However, Francis X. Martin had moved to Louisiana years earlier and became the attorney general and later the presiding judge of the Louisiana Supreme Court. All accounts agree that Burns threw a lawyer named Martin into the chilly waters of the Neuse. Many legends and myths and sometimes huge inaccuracies based on the true exploits of Otway Burns would follow after this day.

* * *

There is an old joke with many variations that goes something like this:

Q: What do you call a lawyer at the bottom of the river?
A: A good start.

Maybe that joke started with Otway Burns.

* * *

The days leading up to the dunking had been intense.

Burns, a merchant captain who was known up and down the East Coast as arriving on time and intact and worthy of commanding a premium for his work, was in New Bern to start a new enterprise.

He and a group of local investors had purchased a Baltimore Clipper and refitted it to begin service in what became known as the War of 1812. The United States Navy was stretching to call itself a war-making force, so Congress, out of necessity, had declared it would engage a historically successful enterprise—privateering to compensate for the lack of a competitive fighting force. Letters of marque were being issued for independent contractors to arm ships and gather crews to make war and raids on British shipping. Captains and crew would split any captures and prizes with the government.

In his late 30s at the outbreak of the war, Burns was too old to begin a navy career and too disposed in his ways to serve under the command and whims of others, especially those without his skill in mastering a ship or his drive and determination to fight. This is not to mention that there were fewer than 25 warships in the American navy, so there would not have been a command available even if he had desired to go that route. Privateers were going to have to do most of the work at sea for the still young United States. Burns also considered himself a patriot ready and willing to serve his country. It certainly didn't hurt that he also loved a dollar.

His ship, renamed the *Snap Dragon*, had come to New Bern (usually spelled Newbern in those days) to finish outfitting and recruiting sailors. The problem was that many of the politicians in town considered privateering to be the same as piracy. They did not want their town attracting rogues and thieves and murderers—North Carolina's coast had a reputation for harboring of pirates in the 1700s, chief among them was Edward Teach, also known as Blackbeard. New Bern was a respectable and important place. Town leaders also feared an invasion or bombardment by the British navy, as there was little defense and no hope of any coming in the near future—the governor and the president had already said as much. States were going to have to fend for themselves and the somewhat backward North Carolina had little money or weaponry to offer.

Since the federal government legally permitted privateering, the local leaders had to come up with other means to remove these raiders. Ironically, they were not above questionable, law-skirting practices and convinced many of Burns' new recruits to borrow money before they set sail to make sure they could take care of any expenses and debts they might incur before they return from their voyage and

1. A Lawyer in the Neuse River

were able to get their shares of loot. What would happen, they told the men, if there was no loot to split?

The crewmen were happy to take advantage of these newly offered credit terms. However, they had placed their faith in the wrong people and did not foresee their notes and debts being immediately recalled. The conniving moneylenders had warrants quickly issued for the arrest of a large number of Burns' men and authorities planned to remove the crewmen from the *Snap Dragon*.

Burns was having none of this. In the strongest terms, he had made it clear that he was the only sovereign on the *Snap Dragon*, and no one would board his ship without his permission. The town's leaders decided to call his bluff or what they thought was a bluff.

A boatload of constables pushed off from shore and rowed toward the *Snap Dragon*, ready to take into custody the debtors and any others they might decide needed a lesson while serving under this former merchant captain who seemed to consider himself above local law.

Burns saw them coming. As the deputies made their way toward the ship, they doubtless announced their intentions, and it's likely that threats were issued from the deck of the *Snap Dragon*. What happened next is where legend and fact continued their entanglement with Captain Burns.

The officers were told to turn around and go back to shore and that they would not be allowed on the ship. The crew gathered on deck to see how their new commander was going to handle things.

The constables were determined and continued on, not realizing the storm they were riding into. One legend says that shots were fired at the rowboat, which caused a scramble away from the bullets and opened a space for small arms fire to put enough holes into the craft to sink it. This story seems unlikely, as no injuries and no drownings were reported, and the constables were too far out to swim back to shore. It also does not fit the Burns profile that he would use deadly force against law enforcement, regardless of principle, not to mention the dangers of using relatively inaccurate pistols of the era in such a way.

Captain Otway Burns

Another far more likely report said that Burns allowed the boat to draw alongside his ship and then crewmen used gaffes and poles and hooks, and perhaps hanging from ropes and nets, managed to overturn the boat and dump its passengers into the river. It was in this moment—too late—that it became apparent they had underestimated Burns, as no offer of help or lifeline was thrown to the floundering men. They were forced to crawl onto the bottom of the overturned boat to avoid drowning and wait for rescue from those onshore.

It seems a pretty good bet they had to listen to hours of catcalls and derision from the men of the *Snap Dragon*, who had now learned they were under the command of no ordinary merchant and certainly a man who did not compromise once he'd made a decision.

This might also explain why, despite being in downtown New Bern when he confronted Martin, no attempt was made to impede, stop, or arrest Burns. One newspaper said that Burns had "finally broke the constables."[3]

* * *

New Bern officials were enraged that they'd been defied, while many of the local citizens and perhaps those who anticipated offering trade goods in their stores that might be acquired through privateer auctions found quite a bit of humor in the episode. That incident led to politicians being bolder in their calls for expulsion and is what put Martin in his unfortunate position. Calling the privateers pirates was the popular slight, one they thought would resound with the townspeople. It was true that many pirates got their starts as agents of the state and some took advantage of wars to "legally" practice their trade.

Sea captains of this era were judge, jury, and executioner regarding all charges, real and imagined, on board their vessels. A temper coupled with physical strength and a fearless streak were useful tools for a ship's commander, and it was now clear that Burns was not a man to back down or suffer attacks on his honor. As it turned out, the

1. A Lawyer in the Neuse River

New Bern adventures were just foreshadowing. Soon, Burns would leave town, and the exploits on his first voyage brought him fame and notoriety, and not even local politicians could curb his growing popularity among the people.

* * *

Otway Burns, 37 when the War of 1812 started, became one of the most successful privateers of the War of 1812 and its first naval hero despite the fact he was not technically in the navy. Historian Edgar Stanton Maclay compared him favorably to the much better known John Paul Jones. Burns' ship, the *Snap Dragon*, spent 358 days at sea. Exploits of sailing through storms and righting his ship as it appeared destined for the bottom of the Atlantic made their way back to America. He sometimes surprised enemies by sailing right at them and taking fire or running away with his speedy ship when necessary and firing a "kiss-off" warning shot when safely out of range. There were also legends later disproved, including one involving the infamous case of Theodosia Burr, the daughter of former vice president and Alexander Hamilton killer Aaron Burr, who disappeared at sea during the conflict while sailing from South Carolina to New York.

The war made Burns wealthy, and in its aftermath, he intended to grow that wealth. He started several enterprises and invested in the businesses of many of his friends. Those who served with him help spread stories and create legends. He built ships at his docks that made history.

He was elected to the state legislature at the peak of his popularity and served for over a decade. However, what made him loved by many also made him hated by the few, but the few had more money and more power. Burns was determined to go his own way and considered that to be the unequivocal right way—and by championing the rights of all North Carolinians, he cost himself much political support from the rich and influential in his local circle.

As his political fortunes turned, so did his personal ones. He

Captain Otway Burns

made some big bets that cost him, and money he'd loaned to friends became uncollected debts. The people he thought were friends were no longer interested in him.

Things got so bad that he would have been homeless and destitute if not for the actions of a sitting president who remembered and appreciated his war service. By the time he died, he was considered a broken, drunken bar-brawling has-been, not the colorful local legend he once was. The same traits that had made him rich and powerful cost him dearly when he hit hard times, and it took nearly half a century for that reputation to be restored.

But oh, what stories were created in the life of Otway Burns.

2

Early Life on the Water

Otway Burns, Jr., was born in 1775 in Queen's Creek, near the port of Swansboro (spelled Swansborough until the Civil War) in eastern North Carolina. Swansboro is in Onslow County, about 28 miles southwest of Beaufort, just south of the coastal area commonly referred to as the Outer Banks. Otway's parents, who married in 1768, were Otway Sr., a merchant and tavern keeper, and Lisanah Spooner Burns. Lisanah was from nearby Bear Banks.

Otway Jr. had an older brother, Francis II, named after his paternal grandfather, as well as four younger sisters: Susannah, Mary Ann, Elizabeth, and Experience. Francis Burns, Sr., had emigrated from Glasgow, Scotland, near an area that produced the poet Robert Burns and American naval hero John Paul Jones. He settled in the area around the New River in 1734 but later moved to a plantation that overlooked Bogue Sound in the front and Queen's Creek to the south. Grandfather Francis married Mary Otway in 1744. Otway Sr. was born in 1750 and died in 1797. Lisanah passed the same year.

The first modern European contact in the area might have been in 1524 with Giovanni da Verrazzano's voyage. The first documented settlers—English, Scottish, African, Welsh, and French—came to the Swansboro area in 1713[1] at the site of an Algonquian Indian village at the mouth of the White Oak River. They moved down from New England, Maryland, Virginia, and northeast North Carolina. Originally, the port was called Week's Wharf, then Bogue, and after that, New Town.[2]

On April 7, 1730, Issac and Jonathan Green, brothers from Falmouth, Massachusetts, bought 441 acres from Ebenezer Harker who had emigrated from Boston. Later that year, Harker bought Craney Island, which would be renamed Harker's Island by his heirs when he passed. In 1734, Onslow County was formed out of New Hanover, where the bustling port of Wilmington is located. The county was named for Sir Arthur Onslow, the British Speaker of the House of Commons. The area where the New and White Oak Rivers come together was an excellent location for early shipbuilding. In 1757, Theophilus Weeks was appointed inspector of exports for Bogue Inlet and opened an inn and boarding house. By 1770, he had started a town with six streets and forty-eight 60-by-200-foot lots, the first of which sold the next year. Week's Point or Week's Wharf was the only town between Beaufort and Wilmington along the North Carolina coast.[3]

During the American Revolution, a warehouse was established at the mouth of the White Oak River to supply patriot forces with mostly salted beef and pork. The British blockade reduced the availability of salt, so several saltworks were set up, and privateers began operating out of the port and a military company was formed.[4]

Onslow County was a challenging place to live in the late 18th century. The heat was oppressive, and travel was "disagreeable" as the roads were mostly white sand, often hiding tree roots, which took a toll on horses and riders alike. George Washington visited the area on his famous southern tour in 1791 and called it "the most barren country … [that he] had ever beheld."[5]

Swansboro was later incorporated as a colonial port on May 6, 1783, by the North Carolina General Assembly: "The said village of New Town shall be and is hereby erected into a town by the name of Swannsborough." The town was named for Samuel Swann, who was Speaker of the North Carolina House of Commons from Onslow County. Swann represented the county from 1738 to 1762. He was a surveyor, lawyer, and editor of *Swann's Revival* and was reported as the first surveyor to cross the Great Dismal Swamp while locating the North Carolina–Virginia line.[6] In 1786, the territory trading through the Bogue, Bear, and New River inlets was separated from

2. Early Life on the Water

the port of Beaufort and assigned into Swannsborough, a new port of entry.[7] The name would later be shortened to Swansboro in 1877.

Shipbuilding made Swansboro prosper; between the Revolution and the War of 1812, at least 23 ships were built in the county, and during the War of 1812, two schooners and a 600-ton craft were built.[8] When shipbuilding declined, lumber and naval stores such as tar, pitch, turpentine, and rosin picked up. Other exports included pickled beef, pork, lumber, and slaves.[9] As those industries slowed, commercial fishing grew, and during World War II, there was a boost from nearby newly built Camp Lejeune in Jacksonville. Tourism was the next boom, as the town sits across from what would become the Intercoastal Waterway and Hammocks Beach State Park.

The Burnses attended the Presbyterian church and were well-regarded in the community. Otway Jr. had little formal education[10] but acquitted himself with reading and math. He knew he would need skill and education to follow the path that interested him most as a young man—seafaring. Swansboro and nearby Beaufort, as well as Wilmington (called Brunswick at the time), were key ports in North Carolina, along with Bath, Roanoke, and Currituck, and sailors passed through from all over the world. Otway Sr. was also into shipping, and Otway Jr. learned from him and spent time at the docks listening to stories and gaining as much knowledge as he could. He wasted no time learning to sail skiffs in the Bogue Sound. He quickly became known for his skill, and in 1806 when Burns was 31, the Onslow County Court bound an orphan to him to study navigation.

By the time Otway Jr. reached his early 30s, he was sailing ships on the East Coast as a merchantman. Burns operated a coaster, or swallow-hulled ship, designed for navigating reefs and going where larger oceangoing vessels cannot. He worked from North Carolina all the way up to Portland, Maine, and down to the Caribbean. He inherited land and slaves from his father but in 1808 assigned his property to Francis II to pursue his sailing career.

On July 6, 1809, he married Joanna Grant, a cousin who had

been a neighbor since they were children. Grant was the daughter of Colonel Reuben Grant, a prominent citizen of Onslow County who commanded the local colonial troops during the revolution and filled roles as a priest, sheriff, planter, merchant, attorney, and legislator. The Grants were well-to-do, and there were at least enough reservations about the marriage that Joanna required a prenuptial property agreement before agreeing to marry Burns.[11] Joanna was 23; Otway was 34.

Burns' career expanded as did his reputation for dependability, and soon he was operating out of Beaufort, New Bern, Baltimore, Philadelphia, New York, and Boston, as well as Swansboro and Portland and as far south as the West Indies. Burns was known for his mastery at the helm, being on time, his handling of crews, being honest, and never losing cargo. This allowed him to get a premium for what he hauled. He and Joanna bought Lot #6 in Swansboro in 1810 from Joanna's brother Solomon Elliott Grant and built a house between Front and Water Streets (later, when they moved, the house became part of a shipyard). The description of the lot describes it as bordered on the north by Water Street, on the west by Main Street, and on the south by Front Street and extending the lines across Front Street to include a sizable piece of land between Front Street and the White Oak River. The deed also mentions that a house already occupied the upper portion of the lot.

Burns also entered a key partnership with his good friend Dr. Edward Pasteur, a physician, planter, and political heavyweight from New Bern in neighboring Craven County. Pasteur backed Burns' trading ventures and that partnership later continued and expanded when war broke out.

New Bern was founded in 1710 when 400 immigrants from Switzerland and the German Palatinate arrived in the New World. Many were refugees because of famine, war, religious persecution, or economic difficulties and migrated to London. They were recruited there by Baron Christoph von Graffenried, who was a member of the

2. Early Life on the Water

Swiss group planning a new settlement. They arrived in Virginia and made their way overland from the James River and arrived in September of that year at the junction of the Trent and Neuse Rivers. Von Graffenried and English explorer John Lawson cofounded the town that became known as New Bern. A settler named Christen Janzen wrote of the area, "It is almost wholly forest, with indescribably beautiful cedar wood, poplars, oaks, beech, walnut, and chestnut trees."[12] Within a year, the community was thriving.

However, in 1711, the Tuscarora War broke out with the local Indian tribe. New Bern was where the Native town of Chattoka once stood. Lawson explored much of the area and had good relationships with many of the Native tribes. Lawson and von Graffenried, along with two slaves, were captured. The Indians were upset about recent mistreatment at the hands of settlers and Lawson argued with them. The men were condemned to death, although they did not understand for what reason. Von Graffenried offered help and warned of retribution if he was killed and managed to talk his way into a release. He was told that Lawson would not be spared. Lawson was tortured and killed as the baron was allowed to escape.[13] The war raged for two years with over 100 settlers dying, and some fled to Bath. Virginia offered little help, but South Carolina did, even sending some Indian fighters who hoped to capture slaves with a victory. The Tuscarora were eventually defeated near Snow Hill, North Carolina, in 1713.

New Bern boomed after the revolution, doubling in size from the 1770s to the 1790s and by 1800 was the largest city in the state. It served as the state capital from 1770 to 1792. Merchant wharves were clustered on the Trent River shoreline, and there was shipping traffic from the West Indies, Philadelphia, New York, New England, and Europe. There was a distillery, a tannery, shipwrights, wheelwrights, artisans, cabinetmakers, tailors, silversmiths, slaves, sailors, lawyers, merchants, and even the first bookseller in North Carolina located in the town.[14]

Pasteur and Burns had a long history together, and the doctor was no wallflower, leading his own adventurous life. Pasteur was a wealthy, well-regarded man who had many interests and invested in several local enterprises. When George Washington visited New Bern on his southern tour in April 1791, Pasteur, captain of the New Bern Volunteers and the state's assistant U.S. marshal, was among the Masons from the St. John's Lodge No. 2 who met with him. There was a parade, a public dinner, a 15-gun salute, an exclusive ball at the governor's palace, and public speeches from local dignitaries during the visit.[15]

Pasteur earned some fame and notoriety as the second for former Governor Richard Dobbs Spaight in his infamous duel with Congressman John Stanly on September 5, 1802, behind the Masonic Hall in New Bern. It was an event that had ripples throughout the state's history, including passage of a strong anti-dueling law. Spaight and Stanly had been political rivals for two years. Spaight was the first native-born governor of the state (1798–1801), served in the Revolution, was a member of the General Assembly, was a representative to the Continental Congress, and a signer of the Constitution. Stanly was the son of John Wright Stanly, who moved to North Carolina and married Ann Cogdell, daughter of a leading New Bern family. He made his fortune by outfitting privateers during the revolution, but he helped supply provisions and weapons for which he was never paid. The two men ran against each other for Congress in 1800, and Stanly stated in a handbill that Spaight "pursues the crooked policy of occasionally being on both sides." Stanly won the race, and in 1802 they faced off again. Stanly once again went on the attack, and Spaight finally decided he'd had enough. The former governor demanded satisfaction by sending a note to his rival via Pasteur. Stanly's second was former state representative Edward Graham. Stanly was in poor health at the time of the duel after recently falling from his carriage. Stanly questioned Spaight's loyalty and Spaight put out a handbill during a "paper war" between the two men that called Stanly "a liar and a scoundrel." Stanly said of Spaight's words that they were "a direct attack on my character and one I will not suffer any man to make with impunity."[16]

2. Early Life on the Water

As time went on, Stanly tried to work around the duel and still preserve both men's honor. He offered a public explanation, wrote a second and third letter, and offered to publish them in New Bern's *North Carolina Gazette*. Spaight rebuffed all attempts at reconciliation. Accounts show that about 300 spectators showed up for the 5:30 p.m. duel, and what ensued highlighted the ultimate consequences of what now most consider the absurd practice of dueling.

Both men missed on their first shots. On the second shots, Spaight grazed Stanly's collar, and the spectators pleaded for the men to call a truce and end it with honor intact. Spaight refused. Another round of shots missed, and again, many in the crowd urged the men to call a truce and attempted to stop the proceedings. Pasteur then threatened to shoot anyone who interfered with the completion of the duel.[17]

On the fourth round, Spaight was struck in the side. Friends rushed him home and called in a doctor, but there was nothing to be done. He died the next day. Stanly was charged with murder. In November of that year, the General Assembly created a law to prevent dueling. It prohibited the participants from ever holding public office, allowed for a fine, and for the survivor to be executed. It's worth noting that Stanly's brothers Richard and Thomas both died from wounds received during duels and at least one of John Wright Stanly's grandsons took part in a duel. In 1803, Stanly escaped trial when he was issued a pardon by Governor Benjamin Williams after the state legislature refused to grant him one.

John Stanly's son Edward went on to be a congressman and was appointed by Abraham Lincoln as military governor of eastern North Carolina during the Civil War. John Stanly's grandson Lewis Armistead was a Confederate general who was killed at Gettysburg.

Dr. Pasteur's role in the duel scandal did not hurt his prospects as his prominence continued to rise in New Bern. On March 3, 1809, he was appointed colonel of the Third Regiment of infantry when President Thomas Jefferson signed his commission. He also served as adjutant general of North Carolina (essentially head of the state's national guard) but later resigned his officer's commission in 1810. He begged the legislature to arm the militia, but they refused, and so he resigned to take a commission in the army. Pasteur continued to practice medicine and invest in several local ventures in the New Bern area. He and Burns profited from their shipping operation, and Burns saw his standing in the community rise. Pasteur owned multiple plantations, one of which was bounded by Batchelor's Creek and intersected by Blackman's and McCrohon's Creeks and had several wharves and landings.

Pasteur made one attempt at politics, running against Stanly in the 1814 state House of Commons race. The campaign was "marred by disturbances created by sailors on a privateer and a dispute over black suffrage that favored Stanly."[18] Stanly won a close election, 132–104.

In 1810, Joanna Burns had the couple's only child, Owen. Burns was gone most of the time and saw neither his wife nor child often, which would contribute to marital issues later.

Problems with Great Britain escalated over this time, as British ships—as well as the French—were stopping and boarding United States vessels and "impressing" or essentially kidnapping sailors. This had been going on for years and the United States had even fought the Quasi-War with France prior to this escalation. The British needed men for their navy in the European war and claimed these prisoners were deserters. Although some likely were, many were American citizens with no connection to the British navy.

When war broke out, Burns had made a voyage from New York to Portland and started considering what his role in the coming conflict might be. There wasn't much of an American navy and no chance of Burns being granted command of a ship. He was too patriotic to consider sitting it out or running a vulnerable merchantman for the British navy to pick off. He had much to offer the American war effort. One historian described Burns as "of big, strong frame,

2. Early Life on the Water

tireless endurance, acute active mind, courage, steady nerve in danger, quick temper, good judgment and iron will which have compelled obedience."[19] That, however, opened up an enormous but risky opportunity—outfitting a privateer.

3

War Comes with Britain

CONGRESS DECLARED WAR ON Great Britain on June 18, 1812. America was not united in going to war. In Otway Burns' North Carolina, three of the state's congressional representatives voted against the declaration. The war had been brewing because America wanted to remain neutral and trade with all the warring European countries without taking sides. In 1793, President Washington issued the Neutrality Proclamation, which stated that the United States would "pursue a conduct friendly and impartial toward the belligerent powers."[1] The belligerent powers he referred to were Napoleon I of France and Great Britain.

Although the Korean War is often called the Forgotten War, the War of 1812 could be called that or, at the very least, the Overlooked War. Most Americans have vague notions as to what the war was about because it isn't covered in depth in schools. And to be fair, it isn't exactly clear without close inspection. Many Americans might mention that the "Star-Spangled Banner" was written by Francis Scott Key or that the Battle of New Orleans was fought after peace had already been declared. Some might recall the British burning the White House and several other buildings in Washington, D.C. Few people could articulate what the causes of the war happened to be. The war could have and should have been avoided. Political intrigue, pride, and slow communication were formidable contributors.

The Jay Treaty of 1795 between Great Britain and the United States was taken as an act of betrayal by the French, as it shifted trade away from the ally that had helped the Americans win independence. There had been no trouble with France until the French

3. War Comes with Britain

Revolution, but things changed when King Louis XVI, who had sent ships and troops to swing the course of the American Revolution, was executed by his former subjects. The American government felt that the treaty signed between the two countries in 1778 was no longer valid. The French went to war with Britain and Spain and wanted the United States to help open another front. Many colonists disliked the French because they were mostly Catholic; didn't come as settlers to make a new life in the New World but only to hunt and trade, make a profit, and return home; and had little interaction with other colonists. When the Americans showed they wouldn't take sides, the new French government issued privateer commissions, and the French navy started taking American cargoes, impressed sailors, and seized ships as prizes if they could declare the ships were trading with France's enemies. Secretary of State Thomas Jefferson, one of the leading Francophiles of the time, warned the French that these actions were violations of U.S. neutrality, but he was ignored. The French went so far as to meddle in U.S. federal elections and wanted to get Washington out and Jefferson in as president. When John Adams was elected president, the French Directory responded with an order to treat American ships as the enemy and issued a decree that they could capture neutral ships carrying British goods. Almost every ship had some type of British-manufactured item onboard. They also claimed that any American serving under an enemy flag would be considered a pirate and hanged and that any ship without a list of crew and passengers could be taken as a prize.[2] Things got so bad that by June 1798, many of the Southern states feared a French invasion.

The American government established the Department of the Navy in April 1798, and Congress authorized U.S. ships to capture armed French ships off the American coast. They amended the statement to include anywhere on the "high seas" and licensed privateers. The undeclared, so-called Quasi-War with France was underway. The Americans defeated two frigates in the Caribbean, captured over 100 privateers, and recovered over 70 American merchant ships.[3] The war ended in December 1800 with the Convention of Mortefontaine. At this point, France was fighting the second coalition (Britain, Turkey, Austria, and Russia). Tensions flared up again in 1802, partially because there were a lot of Americans in French-settled New Orleans. Jefferson bought as much land as possible from the Indian tribes on the east bank of the Mississippi River and sent James Monroe to Paris to attempt to buy Louisiana and Florida.

Besides being bullied on the high seas by both England and France, Americans also had to deal with the Barbary states in North Africa (Tunis, Algiers, Tripoli). Muslim pirates raided ships and then started demanding bribes, ransoms, and tributes; refusal to pay resulted in the capture of ships and cargo and crews being enslaved or put in prisons. Along with Sweden and Sicily, the United States fought the first Barbary War from 1801 to 1805 and then, during the War of 1812, fought a second three-day conflict in June 1815. The American navy earned decisive victories and ended both conflicts. Soon enough, it would be the British who would up their antagonism of American shipping as times got desperate and their war dragged on.

The War of 1812 was arguably America's most unpopular war in history. The Federalists were unanimous in their opposition of the declaration of war in 1812 and voted against all proposals to raise men and money and to commission privateers. They had no interest in trying to conquer Canada and feared a war with Britain would foster an alliance with France, something else the Federalists opposed. The Republicans favored ties with France over Britain. The war feelings were split along party lines.

The causes can be boiled down to Britain's Orders in Council and Impressment; the desire by some American politicians to conquer Canada, add territory, and rid the British influence over the Native American tribes; the right to free trade as well as the rights of sailors; to preserve the honor of the country; and, in the case of the Republicans, to gather party unity. The Orders in Council were issued by Britain and required all shipments to stop in English ports

3. War Comes with Britain

to be checked to see if they were carrying any military supplies that would benefit France; any ships that didn't comply were subject to seizure. American ships and their cargoes and sailors were targeted.

The War of 1812 is often referred to as a win in American history texts, but it really was a stalemate that saw the United States narrowly avoid a disaster. It has been called the Second War for Independence, and it can't be denied that it certainly reinforced American sovereignty. Four personalities emerged from the war and would later become presidents—James Monroe, John Quincy Adams, Andrew Jackson, and William Henry Harrison. In addition to New Orleans, there were significant wins at Chippewa and Fort Erie and some naval victories. It also marked the eventual end of the Federalist Party.

While both France and Britain were antagonizing American shipping by seizing ships under the guise of stopping supplies going to the enemy, Britain took it to another level. The British greatly increased impressment with the renewal of war in Europe in 1803 and the Americans wanted a permanent settlement of the issue; continuing to allow this unchecked meant that America was not a truly independent country and was being treated as if it were still a colony of the Crown. The British weren't just seizing cargo, but they were also seizing men, claiming them to be deserters or shirkers of duty despite the fact that many "impressed into service" were American citizens. "Prior to 1812, the British captured 917 ships and impressed 6,257 men. The French seized nearly 500 ships [but didn't impress any sailors into service]."[4] This didn't come completely out of nowhere: the growth of U.S. trade led to the recruitment of more sailors, many of whom were British. It's believed that as many as 25 percent of sailors serving on American ships were British, and it was hard to blame them as pay and conditions were much better. American officials had tried to remedy the problem in 1796 by issuing certificates of citizenship, but many sailors lied about their birthplaces to get one, so the papers had little credibility. British press gangs boarded ships at will to reclaim desperately needed men for service in the conflicts in Europe and they weren't choosy—at least 6,000 American citizens were swept up in these actions and it took years of appeal and court cases to sort it out.[5]

Impressment seems like a ridiculous attack on a nation's sovereignty, but it is not as clear cut when viewing the British perspective. The Brits saw a "mortal danger" from the French, who they felt should be seen as an American enemy with Napoleon threatening liberties that the former colonists claimed to be foundational. They couldn't understand U.S. support of the warmongering dictator Napoleon Bonaparte. They were bothered that the United States felt like it had no stake in the European war and that the British navy was the only thing preventing Napoleon from establishing a European empire and that he wouldn't stop after taking British possessions. To them, it seemed obvious that the French leader had eyes on Spanish and American territory in North America as well. The British were also upset that Americans felt they should be able to trade with both sides and profit from the war.

Who was and wasn't a British or American citizen was a cloudy issue. In America, a sailor could become a naturalized citizen after five years of service, no matter where he was born. The British considered any person born in Britain to be a British subject for life, even though they naturalized all immigrants who served two years on a warship or merchant ship. They did not recognize former British subjects as American citizens.

For their part, the British openly operated in U.S. territorial waters within three miles of the coast. British blockades also interfered with American shipping, and the two countries differed on their definitions of "contraband." The United States considered it strictly to be war materiel, but the British definition extended it to include food and supplies, and the two countries could not agree on how to deal with French property on U.S. ships. Sometimes the British paid for the confiscated goods but never what the cargo would have gotten on the open market. There was also the issue of "reexporting," which meant that ships coming from France had to make

3. War Comes with Britain

port in the United States before continuing on to the next port. Negotiations went on over expired treaties, and the Monroe-Pinkney Treaty of 1806 would have renewed the Jay Treaty and made things better but would not have ended impressment—the British felt it was far less risky to offend the Americans than lose a war to Napoleon. It gave relief from reexporting, provided a narrower definition of contraband, allowed for advance notice of blockades, moved British shipping five miles offshore, and reduced duties for U.S. ships in British ports. This treaty also had an insurance clause that Britain had to reimburse vessels that were detained for suspicious goods. The problem was that Jefferson never submitted the treaty to Congress because he thought the French-Russian alliance would win the ongoing war.

There were moments of armed conflict before the war officially started, the most notorious of which was the conflict between the American ship *Chesapeake* and the British *Leopard*. Deserters from a British ship out of Halifax jumped ship at Hampton Roads and enlisted on the *Chesapeake*. The British got word of this and demanded them and three deserters from the *Melampus*. The men from that ship were Americans who had been impressed by the British. On June 22, 1807, the HMS *Leopard* approached the American *Chesapeake* off Cape Henry on the Virginia coast, demanding they be allowed to board the ship looking for deserters from the navy. The *Chesapeake*'s commander declined, and the *Leopard* opened fire, sending three broadsides that resulted in 3 men killed and another 18 wounded. Unable to defend itself, the *Chesapeake* struck its colors, and the British ship took the men it claimed were deserters. To avoid more conflict after the episode, the British government offered to recall the *Leopard* captain, paid reparations, and returned three of the four men it had taken, who were apparently American citizens. The British man was hanged and the Americans imprisoned in Halifax. It took four years to settle the issue.

Jefferson ordered all armed British ships to leave U.S. waters by July 2. James Monroe, the American minister in London, was ordered to settle the matter, which qualified as an act of war.

The Orders in Council and the Berlin Decree (which forbade all commerce and communication with Great Britain) were in effect from 1807 to 1812 and made trade difficult for the United States. Over 900 ships were seized during the time. U.S. trade restrictions in the form of an embargo on Britain and France proved devastating to the American economy and cut imports by 75 percent. In May 1811, the U.S. frigate *President* fired on the British *Little Belt*, killing 9 and wounding 23.

There was also a belief that the English, still smarting from the Revolution and with interests in the New World, were inciting the Indians on the western frontier. Complicating that was the fact that many Americans—including lawmakers—had their eyes on Canada and Florida, believing the former just needed an opening to join America and that the latter was simply inevitable given geography and the makeup of the settlers. Because the British traded with the Indians, Americans blamed them for many of the hostilities. In November 1811, Indiana Governor William Henry Harrison assembled a company of troops and marched to Prophet Town to confront the Shawnee led by Tecumseh. Harrison demanded that the tribe give up the leaders responsible for attacks following a treaty that required the Indians to sell 3 million acres of land to the United States. Tecumseh's brother Tenskwatawa (the Prophet), with 600–700 braves, attacked and a bloody battle ensued. The troops held their ground and burned Prophet Town the next day in what became known as the Battle of Tippecanoe. This battle would later become a key reference in Harrison's presidential campaign, feeding the cry of "Tippecanoe and Tyler, too!"

From December 1811 until April 1812, the Republican-controlled Congress enacted the war program. They sought to double the size of the army by raising the bounty for enlistment from $12 to $31 and a grant of 160 (or more) acres of land per man. They wanted to raise an additional 25,000 regulars and 50,000 one-year volunteers,

3. War Comes with Britain

authorizing the president to call 100,000 militia for six months and $1.9 million was allocated for the purchase of ordnance.[6]

Back in Burns' home state, North Carolina Governor William Hawkins supported the war, as did most citizens. One of the leading hawks was William King of Sampson County, who later moved to Alabama and was elected as the vice president of the United States in 1852 but died before he could take office. Taxes were approved on salt, liquor stills, and slaves. Most of the opposition came from Federalists, who thought that President James Madison was incompetent. Among that group in the state were Representative William Gaston of New Bern; Representative Joseph Pearson of Salisbury; and Edward Pasteur's old nemesis, John Stanly of New Bern. Senator David R. Stone voted for the war but then voted against the tax to support it. He was one of the peace commissioners who went to Russia before he resigned in 1814.

New England was not pro-war and threatened to secede during the war, eventually calling the Hartford Convention of 1814. Federalists became extremely unpopular in North Carolina because of this. However, there were many powerful people in New Bern who opposed the war. This would provide complications for Burns and Pasteur as they tried to outfit and crew their privateer.

Thomas Jefferson's policies from his time in office certainly contributed to the conflict. The "Federalists believed the best way to avoid war was to prepare for it."[7] The army, at the end of 1789, had 840 men; by 1801, it was at 5,400. Coastal forts were repaired and ships were built. In addition, many in Washington had their sights set on Canada and were willing to fight the British over it—they falsely assumed Canadians wanted to break away from the empire and join the American experiment, a theory that couldn't have been more wrong and that would prove to be a gross and costly miscalculation.

At the beginning of the war, there were 6,686 officers and men in the regular army. By the end of the war, there were 38,186 men in the service—all volunteers. North Carolina's Governor Hawkins did his bit to appeal to volunteers and promoted Major William S. Hamilton to colonel and placed him in charge of recruitment. Men were promised "rifle dress ... favorite weapon ... and you will cover yourselves in glory." The pay was $8–$12 a month, with a $124 bounty and 160 acres of land to be awarded after the war. "Hired musicians" would get the highest wages. It is estimated 1,200 North Carolina men served in the war.[8]

There were early frustrations for North Carolina and that is why some areas vulnerable to invasion, such as New Bern, had growing opposition to the war. North Carolina sent an agent to Washington because no defensive preparations or troops seemed to be coming. The agent was told "the state must rely upon her own resources." Madison gave an even more blunt kiss-off as to how much he valued the Old North State when he said, "An absolute protection of everyone is not possible."[9] The state government wasn't much better at offering protection. Officials in 1813 Swansboro, where Burns grew up and learned his trade, asked Hawkins for help because of the vulnerability of the White Oak and New Rivers. They wanted 50 infantry, 50 cavalry, and 2 cannons. The governor was unable to help as the state focused what little money and resources were available on Beaufort and the Cape Fear River area.[10]

The state legislature refused to give the governor permission to purchase military supplies, and North Carolina paid its own way, little by little. The state was not reimbursed by the federal government until 1916.[11]

The British did not believe the Americans would go to war, mostly because they had no army or navy to speak of. In addition to the ground forces listed earlier, the navy was practically nonexistent, possessing shipyards but not a single dock. Administrations had been reluctant to spend money on the military since 1801.[12] Acting U.S. Minister to Britain Jonathan Russell was authorized to arrange an armistice if the Orders in Council, blockades, and impressment issue could be adjusted. Russell was told that he could assure the

3. War Comes with Britain

British that a law would be passed to prohibit employment of British seamen in public or commercial service in the United States.[13]

On June 1, Madison asked Congress for a declaration of war on Great Britain for its threat to "the United States as an independent and neutral nation.... American citizens, under the safeguard of public law and their national flag, have been torn from their country and everything dear to them; have been dragged on board ships of war of a foreign nation and exposed, under the severest of their discipline, to be exiled to the most distant and deadly climes, to risk their lives in the battles of their oppressors, and to be melancholy instruments of taking away those of their brethren." He condemned Britain and said they "hover over and harass our entering and departing commerce ... plundering our commerce in every sea." He also accused the British of encouraging the Indians to wage war on Americans.[14]

On June 16, 1812, the British announced the Orders in Council had been suspended and, a week after that, lifted the blockade and the license plan. Not knowing this, the U.S. House of Representatives voted 79–49 and the Senate 19–13 to declare war on Great Britain two days later.

Across the Atlantic, London was roiling. There was chaos in the British government as Liverpool merchant John Bellingham shot and killed Prime Minister Spencer Perceval as he entered Parliament on May 11. Many efforts were made to stop the war; Governor-General of Canada Sir George Provost asked that if the Orders in Council could be repealed and impressment addressed, could hostilities be suspended, but it was too late. If news had traveled faster, there might not have been a War of 1812.

Tense and tragic times were ahead for the young United States as the war was headed for its shores, and it would take a number of hard dramatic turns over the course of three years.

4.

Privateering

High places in the temple of fame have been justly awarded to very many, who, in the national employment, have achieved exploits not more brilliant, displayed courage not more daring, seamanship not more masterly, coolness in danger not more remarkable than abound in the records of the private armed service. But the brave and patriotic men who adorned that service, instead of being awarded a proud niche in that temple, have encountered neglect, even obloquy. No testimonials of national gratitude have rewarded their blood-bought victories, and their invaluable services in crippling the resources of the common enemy.[1]

—Captain George Coggeshall
Former privateer, writing about privateers in 1856

Shipping was of the utmost importance to the new United States at the turn of the 19th century. Virtually everything the citizens needed or desired—with the exception of lumber—was brought in by ship. Along with agriculture, fishing was also a key industry, and so there were plenty of privately owned ships in ports all along the East Coast. This made conditions ripe for the explosion of privateers when the need arose.

A privateer is a privately owned, armed ship licensed by a government to rob, capture, and/or disable enemy ships during war, with a focus on merchant ships. Critics have long referred to the practice as legalized piracy, but most privateers bristled at that accusation. Some believe the word was created as a combination of "private" and "volunteer."

The United States used privateers during the Revolutionary

4. Privateering

War. Privateer Jean Lafitte, who at times also worked as a pirate, played an important role for General Andrew Jackson at the Battle of New Orleans in the War of 1812. Although John Paul Jones wasn't technically a privateer, his USS *Ranger* acted like one, taking merchant prizes and operating alone. David Porter, Sr.—father of his more famous son who served during the Quasi-War and the War of 1812—served on privateers during the War of Independence. Stephen Decatur, Sr., who also had a more famous naval hero son, Stephen Decatur, Jr., served as a privateer during the revolution and the Quasi-War. Most European countries eventually prohibited privateering with the Declaration of Paris in 1856, but the United States never signed on. The Confederacy employed privateers as well as "commerce raiders" during the Civil War. Perhaps the most famous privateer of all time was Sir Francis Drake, British naval hero of the 16th century, who circumnavigated the globe.

Privateers were essential to the United States' war effort beginning in 1812. In writing about Otway Burns, magazine editor Jim Dean said, "More than any other influence, privateers turned the tide of the War of 1812."[2] Some felt privateers were key to the entire naval campaign by targeting merchants instead of military targets, "as in a voice of thunder" should dictate to Congress how the enemy should be assailed.[3]

Privateering allowed weaker nations to challenge more powerful ones. At the beginning of the War of 1812, the U.S. Navy had 23 ships, while the British navy was arguably the largest and best force on the sea with over 1,000 ships, 800 of which were ready for action or in good order and 100 were already in service in the western Atlantic Ocean. The British did have a problem of their ships being undermanned due to the long wars with France—which is part of the reason impressment was so vital.

Of the 23 ships in the American navy, only 14 were ready for service at the beginning of 1812, and the roster broke down this way:

- There were three 44-gun frigates: the *Constitution*, *United States*, and *President*.
- There were three frigates: *Congress*, *Essex*, and *John Adams*.
- There were two ship sloops: the *Hornet* and *Wasp*.
- There were three brig sloops: the *Argus*, *Syren*, and *Nautilus* and two smaller brigs, the *Enterprise* and *Viper*.
- The brig *Oneida* was stationed on Lake Ontario.
- There were 165 small gunboats.
- There were three frigates ordered to be repaired: the *Constellation*, *Chesapeake*, and *Adams*.
- There were 500 officers and 5,230 men.[4]

There were 517 privateer ships.[5] These "legal pirates" were essential to the American war effort—there was no choice but to employ privateers. The British lost about 2,000 ships during the War of 1812, not counting the Great Lakes campaigns, and privateers were responsible for 1,300 of those.[6] Losses have been estimated at $23,880,000 (over $462,000,000 today) with around 16,000 casualties for the British. One British captain was captured three times, released, captured three more times, and saw ten different privateers.[7] It's fair to say the British feared privateers more than they feared the American navy.

Privateers could take cargo and let the ship go, remove the cargo and crew and destroy the capture, or put a prize crew onboard and try to make it to safe harbor. The crew would then have a hearing to prove that the ship was a legal capture, which could be condemned and sold. Those not proven legal had to be returned to the rightful owners.

North Carolina Supreme Court Chief Justice Walter Clark, who was a speaker at the 1909 monument dedication to Otway Burns many years after his death in his namesake town of Burnsville, North Carolina, thought of the privateers in a different way: They were "simply a volunteer navy, dependent upon its own enterprises for courage and pay." Clark added that taking the war to the wealthy was an underrated factor in the war: "The eminent buccaneers of

4. Privateering

Wall Street wish war to be confined to wounding and killing of sailors and soldiers (who have small interest in the war), but that their own property should be held sacred on the high seas ... the surest way to create a desire for peace among the influential element of the enemy is for the privateer to lay rude hands about their floating wealth."[8]

Many seamen were eager to become privateers as a way to serve in the war but also potentially acquire wealth. Congress declared war in June 1812. They also passed Article Number 1, Section 8, Clause II, which allowed privateers. In the first six months, privateers captured 500 merchantmen and thousands of POWs. Privateers operated off the American coast, in the English Channel, Irish Channel, Bay of Biscay, Spanish coast, Hindustan, Australia, the West Indies, South America, Africa, and even the Arctic Circle.

Baltimore was the center of U.S. activity with 58 privateer ships, followed by New York with 55, Boston with 32, Philadelphia with 14, Portsmouth (NH) with 11, and Charleston with 10. Other ports accounted for over 250. The state counts were higher at 150 for Massachusetts, 112 for Maryland, 102 for New York, 31 for Pennsylvania, 16 for New Hampshire, 15 for Maine, 11 for Connecticut, 9 for Virginia, and 7 each for Georgia and Louisiana for a total of over 500 letters of marque.[9] North Carolina had four: the *Lovely Lass* out of Wilmington; the *Hawk* from Washington; the *Hero* of New Bern, captained by Thaddeus Waterman;[10] and the *Snap Dragon*, commanded by Otway Burns, out of New Bern. During the war, the *Anaconda* from New York used North Carolina as a safe haven. The ship captured *King's Packet*, landed at Edenton, and sent the coins to banks in Tarboro.[11]

The *Yankee* of Bristol, Rhode Island, is often considered by historians as the most successful privateer of the war. It was a 168-ton brig with 14 cannons and 120 men. The ship made six cruises from Nova Scotia to West Africa and even the English Channel. It used three captains during the war and took 40 prizes valued at $5 million.[12] Its biggest prize was the *San Jose Indiano*, which, with ship and cargo, was valued at $600,000. The *Snap Dragon* record wasn't far behind.

Speed was the primary aim of these ships, so they could evade heavily armed British warships. When fleets went out, they went after stragglers. Most carried one long-range gun known as a "Long Tom" and several smaller cannonades. Long guns were accurate but were heavy and required lots of powder. Carronades didn't have a long range but could do a lot of damage up close and were a fraction of the cost of long guns. Ships ranged from small schooners to three-masted, heavily armed warships. The North Carolina coast was a popular hunting ground for privateers, as the North Carolina ports were easy to slip into and escape because larger ships could not follow. Edenton, New Bern, Beaufort, and Wilmington were the main suppliers.

Privateers could be a sloop, schooner, brig, or bark, and the spars had to be sound to hold as much sail as possible and the ship maintained in good condition to be able to hold up under great strain. Some ships in the tropics had copper sheathing on the bottom. The ships also wanted to appear as much like a merchantman from a distance as possible. That's one reason they rarely carried many guns. Another reason was that prolonged firing could tear apart these usually smaller and lighter ships. The *Skunk*, a successful privateer during the American Revolution, had only two guns. Since they carried only a few guns, captains were always looking for an upgrade, and often, one of the first things taken off a capture was the guns.

Privateers had to meet the "particulars of the government" to operate. A commission and letter of marque and reprisal was required and had to be renewed prior to each voyage. Ship owners applied through local customs officials for these documents for each cruise. This was the official "license" to attack enemy shipping. Getting a letter was not hard unless the captain or the investors had a "questionable" past. The clamor for letters of marque was "like a gold rush as everyone wanted to cash in."[13] The letters could limit the area where a privateer could operate or they could be unlimited,

4. Privateering

but they almost always had a time limit. They were no longer valid once peace was declared, and any prizes taken after that point had to be returned. Voyages were not long. Captains traveled light out of necessity, and being laden with captured goods carried its own risk, not to mention the reduction of crew members on the ship after dispatching prize crews. Letters had to be protected at all costs because if they were captured by the enemy without a letter, they would be hanged as pirates. A letter guaranteed treatment as a POW. That meant horrific living conditions and a potential death sentence but at least not at the end of a rope.

Owners of the ships had to give bonds and observe regulations. The bond had to be for the value of the vessel as insurance against possible future claims and legal fees. The commanders and crews took an oath to adhere to the rules as well as an oath of allegiance. Upon their return from each voyage, the ship had to submit a journal of each day's activities, including the name and value of each capture, verified by the commanding officer. The ship's logs had to be delivered to a local officer when the privateer returned to port that included a complete list of captured ships, confiscated cargo, and the location, date, and time of all actions. All captures that weren't burned or ransomed out of necessity at the time—the need to escape an enemy or not having an adequate prize crew, for example—were to be turned over to the government. A court of admiralty then determined who owned the vessel and whether it was a legal capture. At that point, the prize was condemned and approved to be sold at auction. The cargo was usually auctioned within 30–90 days after arrival at the docks, and import duties were deducted from the proceeds and a small percentage was reserved as a pension for disabled sailors and for the widows and children of crew members killed in the line of duty. Of what was left, sometimes less than 60 percent of the gross value, the owners of the ship split 50–50 with the crew.

There was money to be made, more than a low-level sailor with little to no education could expect in any other jobs of the time. The navy offered prize money but not like the opportunities aboard

Captain Otway Burns

a privateer. Crews usually got wages and a share and $1,000 was a common amount for a tour, a small fortune at the time. Government ships also got prize money but rarely on the level of privateers.[14] Privateer captains and crew had to be bold and take risks, as coming up empty meant no pay. There was a distinct method of parsing out the proceeds on a privateer. Everything was divided into "lays," usually totaling 64. The ship's owner and the captain usually took half; the officers and men took the other half on a sliding scale. There was an extra payment made for sailors who died or lost an arm or leg. If a man was considered to show cowardice in action, he forfeited his lay. All onboard signed articles of agreement.[15] There was also a private licensed vessel called a letter of marque, which primarily carried cargo but could also capture enemy shipping when the opportunity arose.

Life on a privateer was much easier than on a military ship of the line. Captains typically had little trouble recruiting sailors, only needing to avoid naval deserters. Discipline was not as strict, but the captain was all-powerful—his orders could not be appealed. This was yet another distinction from piracy. Ideal crew members also had to cut from somewhat different cloth than commercial workers as well; "a sullen crew was okay on a merchantman, but [on a] privateer [a member] needed alertness, smartness, and a willingness to fight."[16]

Crews were large and holds were mostly empty, especially at the beginning of a voyage, so the work was spread around and not as hard, although officers tried to keep the men occupied. The crew numbers dropped as a cruise went on as men were needed to man prizes and get them back to a home harbor. Sometimes privateers returned to their ports with one-tenth of the original crew. Sometimes having a number of armed men on deck, appearing ready to board and fight, discouraged resistance from merchant targets—men who were not being paid enough to put their life on the line for cargo. The crew also had to be ready after a capture to load the hold quickly and to guard prisoners.

During the War of 1812, a bounty was paid for POWs, but most

4. Privateering

captains wanted to get rid of them as soon as possible. In addition to the cost of feeding them, there was a real danger of too many prisoners being able to overthrow the small crews. The government had to raise bounties substantially to encourage privateers not to release captives. The amount was changed at times but was generally $20 per POW. In March 1813, Congress offered half the value as a prize for any burned, sunk, or destroyed armed British vessel. This meant just about every ship flying English colors after the war started, as most had some type of weapon for self-defense. Later in August of the same year, the bounty was raised to $25 per prisoner, pensions were added for wounded privateer crew members, and duties on captured goods were reduced by one-third.

Some privateers worked in pairs. One would occupy the escort, while the other chased after the merchant ship. Coffee and sugar were the most desired cargoes. Good weather made for slim pickings, but bad weather offered opportunities. Some merchant ships were fast and others were heavily armed. Many privateers, like Otway Burns, fitted their ships for speed and the *Snap Dragon* was among the swiftest. Fast ships that avoided the British navy and impressment before the war made great privateers. One prize target for privateers was government mail packets, which often carried specie and payrolls but were generally fast and well-armed.

Privateers operated under a simple set of tactics. They favored fast ships that could catch slow merchants and outrun larger warships. They did not want long engagements as they were lightly armed as far as cannon, and as the war went on, merchants began arming themselves more heavily. Once in range, instead of shelling the other ship, privateers worked to get close enough to board and finish the job in hand-to-hand combat. Prolonged fighting or shelling could damage the prize and cut profits or, worse, could damage the privateer ship, which could end the cruise and be financially devastating. Even fast privateers couldn't always get away and sometimes had no choice but to fight better armed warships.

There were risks in combat, but even after a big prize, there were no sure things. Of the 2,000 prizes captured by U.S. privateers, about 750 were recaptured by the British. Some privateers went broke.[17]

There were other dangers besides the hazards of the sea and combat. Prison and prison ships offered horrendous conditions, and the worst among the British was a place called Dartmoor, located 15 miles northeast of Plymouth and later best known as the setting for *The Hound of the Baskervilles*. By the end of 1814, the prison held 6,000 Americans.[18] Months after the war ended, in April 1815, there was a massacre of American POWs when guards fired into a mass of agitated prisoners, killing 6 and wounding over 60.[19]

Whereas many—then and now—viewed privateers as no different from pirates, former privateer George Coggeshall, who wrote a book about American privateers, took exception. He said that thinking privateers weren't serving their country "is a base slander upon the good name and fame of these worthy and gallant defenders of their country's rights and of its honor and glory."[20] Privateers were "not legal pirates, they were legal business enterprises … owned by an individual or group to assist the war effort and make a profit."[21]

The public followed the activities of the privateers almost like sports fans with their teams today. Newspapers reported regularly on the prizes and arrival of the ships in port. Not only were merchants excited to get goods to sell, but also the American public welcomed these small victories in a war that offered few.

One of the most famous publications for reporting privateer news was the *Weekly Register* in Baltimore, commonly known as *Niles' Register* or the *Niles Weekly Register*, after its owner and publisher, Hezekiah Niles. Niles felt that the U.S. Navy should follow the privateer path and focus on damaging British merchant shipping than going toe-to-toe with the better armed and equipped navy. The publisher also advocated for the navy to build smaller ships because they could be built faster, and he felt the success of the privateers proved him out. He also thought every enemy ship should have been destroyed to prevent the possibility of recapture by the British.

To make the "official report" in his paper, Niles had a set of

4. Privateering

criteria that had to be met: The majority of a merchant's merchandise had to be removed by the privateer or the vessel burned, or the prize crew had to make it to a friendly port for condemnation. The fact that Burns had such poor luck with prize crews might be why he isn't regarded as one of the top privateers from the war—Niles had his ship ranked 15th based on 22 captures that met the criteria.[22]

Niles' criteria created a different ranking of the war's privateers than is commonly seen in the work of historians. He broke it down this way:

1. The *Surprize* had 37 captures working the British and Irish Channels, then Canada, and then returned to the British coast. Its crew often burned, destroyed, or sank its captures—almost 50 percent of them. The *Surprize* ran aground on the New Jersey coast in 1815 and was destroyed by the surf.
2. The *Prince-de-Neufchatel* had 34 captures, mostly in the British and Irish Channels. It is most famous for taking on the HMS *Endymion* off Nantucket. The *Endymion* had over 30 guns and 300 men, while the *Neufchatel* had 17 guns and 33 men. The privateer survived but was captured in December 1814.
3. The *Yankee*, regarded by many as the most successful privateer of the war, had 32 captures. The ship worked around Canada, then toured West Africa, which was unusual. It sent all prizes to the United States, but in one capture of a slave ship, it set the slaves free on the African continent.
4. *America* had 31 captures, primarily on the British coast, and sent all prizes to New England.
5. *Comet* had 30 captures while working the West Indies and sent its captures to southern ports, primarily Wilmington, North Carolina.
6. The *Fox* (of Portsmouth; there were at least two other privateers named the *Fox*) worked on the coast of New England for 28 captures. It sent prizes to France and Norway.

Captain Otway Burns

Perhaps most remarkable is that the ship went into action in 1812, made seven cruises, and was still active at the end of the war.

7. The *Caroline* had 28 captures, which were mostly sent to Charleston.
8. *Savoy Jack* had 27 captures and sent its prizes to St. Mary's, Georgia, Savannah, and Charleston.
9. The *True-Blooded Yankee* had 27 captures and operated out of Brest, France. It once captured and held an island off Ireland for six days and a town in Scotland for seven days.
10. The *Scourge* was out of New York and took 26.5 prizes (it shared one) but started from Bordeaux, France, working as a pair with the *Rattlesnake*, another well-known ship.[23]

Burns went on three cruises: two in the West Indies and one in the Nova Scotia–Newfoundland area. He ranged from Cape Farewell at the southernmost point of Greenland to Cape San Roque, the easternmost point of Brazil. Investors got a return of 8–12 percent.[24] Burns captured 42 ships and cargoes valued at over $4 million, in addition to taking hundreds of prisoners, which carried a bounty of $10 each, later $20 and $25 (although most prisoners were dropped off at the next available port).

Historians have often referred to Burns as "a terror to all the British in American waters" and that he "conducted a campaign on the ocean in the War of 1812 which, in some respects was on a smaller scale but in other elements on a larger scale than the brilliant exploits of the great naval hero of the Revolution [John] Paul Jones."[25]

5

The First Tour of the *Snap Dragon*

WHEN WAR BROKE OUT ON June 18, 1812, Burns was in Portland, Maine, having arrived from the Pamlico Sound earlier that month. Pasteur accompanied him as he may have on other trips. The pair found out from the crew of another ship that war had been declared. Several privateers were outfitting in Portland and suggested to Burns that he upfit his coaster and join them. It was tempting and Burns also received multiple local offers to buy his ship and have it outfitted as a privateer, with him installed as captain. He was well known and well regarded all up and down the ports of the East Coast, and Maine was no exception. However, he did not think the ship was fast enough, remarking that "speed and spirit"[1] were what mattered most and that his vessel was too slow. Burns began shopping for the fastest ship he could find. He and Pasteur planned to recruit investors back home in New Bern and the surrounding areas.

The pair sailed from Portland to New York as quickly as possible, worried they might get entangled in the impending British blockade of the American coast. Burns and Pasteur found the fast ship they were looking for in New York City that summer. They paid $8,000 (about $175,000 in 2022 dollars) for the 147-ton ship called the *Zephyr* (some accounts say the men purchased a ship called the *Levere*, but it was the *Zephyr*), owned by Jedediah Olcott. At first, Olcott did not want to sell. Pasteur fronted the cash, and the ship was registered in his name. The Baltimore clipper had been built in

Model of the *Snap Dragon* built by Jim Goodwin (courtesy Jim Goodwin).

1808 in West River, Maryland, an area known for making good vessels during that period. The *Zephyr* was 85½ feet long, with a beam of 22½ feet and a depth of 8 feet 8 inches. It was flush decked and sported two masts. Burns was excited about the ship that sat so low in the water that it allowed "anyone to touch the sea with the hand when reaching out of a cabin window."[2]

The ship was narrow with very low bulwarks. Burns had yards fitted to the foremast and possibly on the mainmast as well, which could be put on the deck at short notice when the ship was beating against the wind or replaced when caught in a gale. This move combined the advantages of a fore-and-aft schooner with the square rigging of a brig. They armed the ship with a 12-pound pivot gun and six to eight guns (probably 6-pounders) and carried swivel guns

5. *The First Tour of the* Snap Dragon

on at least two of the three eventual cruises.[3] Small arms, including cutlasses, pistols, muskets, boarding pikes, pickaxes, and blunderbusses, were added for the crew. Most important, the ship was fast, which Burns believed was the key feature for a successful privateer. He sold his coaster and a few of his crew joined him on the new venture.

They renamed the ship *Snap Dragon*, "an animal not dangerous in either sting or bite, but having a suddenness of motion quite startling." The men who served on the ship called her "The Snap."[4] Another story reasons that snap dragon was a play "on the flower's name and an image of a dragonfly that darts unexpectedly across the water."[5] There is a more colorful story of the ship's naming in Ruth Barbour's *The Cruise of the* Snap Dragon, a historical novel based on Burns and his famous ship—it's included in chapter 14, "Legacy of Legends and Lies" in the book you're now reading.

A commission, or letter of marque and reprisal, was issued to Burns and Pasteur in New York on August 8, 1812, and the men took an oath of allegiance to the United States. There is some disagreement among researchers about who sailed the *Snap Dragon* to New Bern—some say Burns, but others like historian Lindley S. Butler say it was Pasteur. In at least one record, Pasteur was listed as "chief owner of the six-gun schooner, the *Snap Dragon*, commanded by Captain Otway Burns."[6] There were five commissions taken out for the ship, the first two in Pasteur's name in 1812 and 1813, the next two by Burns in 1813 and 1814, and the last taken by William Graham of New Bern.

Burns and Pasteur signed on investors Charles Sanders, New Bern merchant Charles G. Ridgely, James B. Carney, Lott Battle, and Bennett Ferrill and reached out to Tarboro for Theophilis Parker and to Edenton for John Miller. William Shepard, of what was then Shepard's Point and is now known as Morehead City, invested as did James McKinley, New Bern merchant John Harvey, New Bern shipbuilder and planter Isaac Taylor, William R. Graham, and Charles Churchill. Investors paid $260 for each of 50 shares for a total of

$13,000. Burns finished the outfitting of the ship in Beaufort at the shipyard of Elijah Pigott.[7]

Upon arrival in New Bern, Burns opened a shipping office and began recruiting crew members at the busy port. New Bern, where the Neuse and Trent Rivers meet, is North Carolina's second oldest city and a former state capital, having been settled in 1710 by Swiss immigrants. Almost 40 percent of the slaves in Craven County were living in New Bern.[8] At one time, it was the largest city in the state and a very busy port and point of trade with entry into the Atlantic Ocean between Norfolk, Virginia, and Wilmington, North Carolina. There was wealth and culture and rapid growth after the revolution and at one point was called the "Athens of the South." There was plenty of skilled labor to be found to man a ship.

Serving on the *Snap Dragon* offered no wages, but it did offer a share of prize money, a smart enticement for a skilled captain to use, and Burns signed on about 40 men. The risk for the crewmen would be one with a grand payout. However, not everyone in town was excited about the Burns and Pasteur enterprise. Despite being well known as a trusted ship's master, local politicians were not pleased to have Burns in town. Despite Pasteur being a prominent figure, it didn't help sway the local leaders. Many were against the war for various reasons, some political but mostly for the fear of a British invasion. This was a legitimate concern as North Carolina's coast and the New Bern area had very little in the way of practical defense, especially against a force as formidable as the Royal Navy. Others were outspoken in their criticism of privateering in general, considering it to be no more than piracy. Burns referred to his opponents as Tories, a disparaging term left over from the American Revolution to refer to British loyalists; Burns essentially considered his opponents traitors.

These men weren't sure how to deal with Burns. They couldn't send him away legally since he and Pasteur had taken all the steps to be licensed and accredited by the government in their enterprise. So they tried to get creative. Many of them convinced sailors to take out loans so they would have cash immediately, taken as security

5. *The First Tour of the* Snap Dragon

expected profits from the voyage. They then called in those debts almost instantly and issued arrest warrants for the debtors. The conspirators were pretty proud of their dirty trick and believed they'd outmaneuvered Burns and solved their problem. (North Carolina didn't abolish imprisonment for debt until 1867.)

Burns informed local authorities that no law enforcement or legal officials would be allowed on his sovereign ship at anchor in the river without advance permission and that included process servers. Officials called what they thought was a bluff to force his hand. They sent six constables out in a rowboat to board the *Snap Dragon* and haul the crew off to jail, hoping to break Burns before he started and send him to another port to operate.

Burns warned the men as they approached that they would not be allowed to draw closer or to board his ship. The constables, feeling their authority and confidence would win the day, pushed on. They wouldn't be the last to underestimate the resolve, temper, and fight in Otway Burns and within minutes found themselves scrambling to crawl onto the bottom of their capsized boat to keep from drowning. Burns had ordered his men to use poles to tip the boat over. One report said that "this frolick finally broke the constables."[9] No arrests were made. The New Bern men behind this ruse clearly had underestimated what type of man they were dealing with and the fighting spirit and resolve he possessed when he felt he was in the right—which was most of the time. They wouldn't be the first or last foes to make that mistake.

Not long after that, a lawyer/historian/anti-war protester with the last name Martin referred to Burns as nothing more than a "licensed robber." Word quickly made its way out to the *Snap Dragon*. The captain had some men row him ashore, where he found Martin and gave the attorney his unanticipated dip in the Neuse River. Burns established that he was not a man to tolerate those who might stand in his way or disparage his honor and good name. Burns boasted a "powerful physique, herculean strength, tireless endurance, dauntless courage and inflexible will."[10] Several accounts of this story name Francis X.

Captain Otway Burns

Martin as the lawyer who went into the river. It made a good story because Francis was a man of note, but isn't true. Francis X. Martin was appointed attorney general of Orleans territory in 1809 and of Louisiana in 1813 and served as a Louisiana Supreme Court justice from 1836 to 1846, eventually taking the "presiding judge" role, the equivalent of chief justice. He'd served in the North Carolina General Assembly during 1806–1807 and printed the newspaper the *North Carolina Gazette*. He'd already left New Bern and the state for some time when the episode took place.[11]

The *Snap Dragon* needed fewer than ten crew members to operate when underway, but additional men were needed for boarding and for prize crews to guide back to port those ships captured. With only 25 men on board and realizing that his time in New Bern wasn't worth the trouble, Burns left the port on October 14, 1812, and headed to Norfolk to finish recruiting. He picked up around 50 sailors and completed his crew.

This is another place where historians don't always agree and 200 years' passing makes things difficult to verify. Although the credit typically goes to Burns and the accounts from crew and early newspapers publications concur, the commissions and legal notices list Pasteur as the commander and William Mitchell as the first lieutenant. Statements executed at sea on December 19, 1812, and again on January 16, 1813, list Pasteur as the captain in reference to prisoners captured. There is a theory that Burns was on board to take over the helm in times of danger. However, the biography by Burns' grandson Walter Francis Burns lists Burns as captain with First Lieutenant Benjamin DeCokely (sometimes recorded as D. Cokely) as his second in command. More support for this comes from the *Snap Dragon*'s first encounter after leaving Norfolk. While in port, Burns met Captain W. Langdon of the 12-gun privateer *Revenge*, who was there to finish assembling his crew as well. The two captains decided to work together, passing through Hampton Roads and sailing down the Chesapeake Bay. It was believed that no man in either crew had any combat experience. But that didn't stop a cocky attitude among

5. The First Tour of the *Snap Dragon*

some men. One of the *Snap Dragon* petty officers named Thompson boasted he would "eat an Englishman alive," and others bragged about their bravery if they had "good fortune to meet a worthy foe."[12] The war was just beginning, and confidence was not short in supply.

Was Pasteur the commander, or because of his reputation, money, and power, was he simply listed on the paperwork with Burns the actual master? There are contradictions among the accounts, for sure. However, it would have made no sense to employ a captain of such skill as Burns possessed, pay him a large share, and then not let him have his work. That would be like benching Michael Jordan or Tom Brady or saving Mike Trout as a pinch hitter. The action reports all attest to Burns' brilliance at the helm and his ferocity in a fight over the course of the war, with no mention of his friend, the doctor, in witness accounts or logs.

Burns went after the first ship he saw, and several of the crew members panicked. During the chase, the *Snap Dragon* left the *Revenge* several miles behind after just two hours. The vessel they pursued turned out to be an American privateer out of Baltimore and caused concerns and grumbling by some of the crew, one of whom remarked that "[the] fool of a boy [Burns] would send them all to prison or the devil, imprudently running alongside a strange vessel before he knew what she was."[13] Some men wanted to wait for the *Revenge*, and others considered themselves "stockholders" with a say in how the ship should operate. Tensions built while the captain and crew awaited more action. It must be remembered that a privateer was not a navy ship with navy discipline and rules. Many members of the crews had danced back and forth across the line of piracy and legitimate work. Pirate crews were accustomed to a measure of democracy for the crew in determining pursuits. Maintaining order was not necessarily a simple task. Burns continued to have to deal with issues among the crew. Thompson had been bragging about his prowess since the beginning of the trip and was attempting to stir the crew up against the officers. During the chase with the *Revenge*, he had disappeared, saying he had important duties in the hold.

Captain Otway Burns

Burns called him out in front of the men for being "loudest in peace" and "stillest in danger." Thompson replied Burns could only get away with such a statement because of his rank as captain. Thompson said, "Captain Burns felt safe in using such language being his superior officer, but he would not do so if ashore and on equality."

Burns faced a tough decision. The temper and his physical gifts and bulldog-like tenacity told him he could take Thompson in a fight, and he mentioned he would "waive all distinctions of grades and called for witnesses that it was considered equal footing."[14] What took place next speaks to the intangible presence of the captain. Instead of challenging Burns, Thompson submitted to the naval discipline of a "genteel flogging" with the end of a rope, which Burns had said was for the good of the discipline of the ship. Later, off St. Matthew's on the Spanish Main, Thompson was put ashore for mutinous talk. Thompson promised revenge and declared that if he ever saw Burns again, he would kill him on the spot. As an interesting footnote, the two crossed paths again in a port after the war and Burns recognized Thompson, recalled the threat, and prepared to defend himself. Instead of attacking, Thompson approached his former captain and asked for forgiveness,[15] begging that the "unpleasant incident" be forgotten.[16]

Not long after, the crew spotted another ship and gave chase, firing a shot across the bow. When they heaved to, it turned out the ship was Spanish, making it an ineligible target even though it's well documented that ships from Spain dodged neutrality laws frequently. It was here, after eight to ten days, that the *Snap Dragon* and *Revenge* parted ways as Burns felt his companion was too slow.

Days later, the *Snap Dragon* made its first capture, taking a British ship with 14 guns but undermanned with only about 10 crewmen. They took the ship to St. Thomas, a British possession in the Virgin Islands (now a U.S. territory). They sent out small boats to scout the harbor and learned that several British merchantmen were preparing to leave. Burns had a plan to cut them out one by one the next day,

5. *The First Tour of the* Snap Dragon

so he took to the other side of nearby Buck Island and disguised the *Snap Dragon* with old sails and hid the guns.

Burns got to showcase his daring as well as his ship handling shortly afterward. The *Snap Dragon* ran into two British man-of-war, including the HMS *Garland*. The *Garland* chased, fired a warning shot, and then just missed with a round from a 32-pounder. Soon, the *Snap* was surrounded by five man-of-war—three to the windward side, two to the leeward side—a perfect trap for the hunters. In one account, Burns had the men run up the Spanish flag, but another report said he used the British colors. In either case, the ruse did not work, and the chase was on.

For two hours, Burn ran a course toward Ship Rock (aka Sail Rock Passage), about 40 miles windward from St. Thomas. The passage was blocked by two British brigs, and it looked like Burns' career as a privateer was going to be a short one. The captain set a course straight for the rock so it couldn't be determined which side he was going to take. The *Garland* continued the chase with a barrage of fire, while the other ships maneuvered to cut the privateer off. At times, the shot from the British ship hit so close that the crew on deck of the *Snap Dragon* was sprayed with sea water. Burns tried to shape a course to get the *Garland* drawing on one sail to take advantage of the size and speed of his ship.

The HMS *Sophie* closed and came abreast of the *Snap Dragon* and prepared to fire grape and round shot. Burns yelled at the crew to lie down on the deck or get below deck and he took the wheel as the blasts came. He spun the ship on an opposite tack and made it pass within a few hundred yards of his adversary. The gun crews on the *Sophie* quickly reloaded but, in their haste, accidentally blew away their own bulwarks. Burns wasted no time in taking advantage of the delay caused by the chaos to make his move—the speedy *Snap Dragon* made a fast getaway. One crewmember put it like this: "[Burns] could [make a ship] walk the waters like a thing of intellect." When he had run the gauntlet and taken advantage of the wind and was safely out of range of the British guns, Burns raised the

Captain Otway Burns

American flag and fired a cannon as a kiss-off salute of goodbye, a gunpowder-backed middle finger of defiance. Burns had flair to go with his mastery of sail. Nightfall ended the chase, but Burns was just getting warmed up.

The next day the HMS *Dominica*, a 15-gun schooner, came after the *Snap* but could not catch her. The wind, usually an ally for the speedy privateer, extracted a cost this time—it took away the jib-boom and the two top masts. The crew made the necessary repairs and started working the St. Croix and St. Thomas areas, took some small vessels and prizes while running into several man-of-war but avoided further damage.

Burns had enough success that the HMS *Nettler* came hunting for him near Tortola in the Virgin Islands. One morning, the chase was on as Burns called, "All hands to quarters." Several officers suggested he run, and the *Nettler* chased for hours. Then began a strange game of cat and mouse. Burns, tired of running, figured he had more men and the same-size ship, so he stopped dead after taking down the light sails. When the *Nettler* closed to about two miles and realized this, it turned and ran for the next 12 hours. Finally, just before nightfall, the *Nettler* passed under the guns of Tortola.

Tortola was set up so that ships could pass one way into the harbor and come out another. Burns raised the British flag as he reached the harbor and sailed under the guns as well—but he didn't realize they were guns. They were painted white and, in the dark, were mistaken for sheep on the hillside. He anchored a half mile off the harbor town.

Burns sent out small boats to try to cut out a few prizes from the anchored ships. He mistakenly pulled up beside the *Nettler*, which immediately answered with musket fire at close range. This drew the attention of the fort and woke the town, which then sent rockets at the *Snap Dragon*. The *Snap Dragon* pulled away, raising a light to guide the smaller boats, which had lost their bearings back in, so they could make an escape. However, the shore battery was using the

5. The First Tour of the Snap Dragon

light to guide fire and find the range, so the men had to extinguish the light and returned fire with the 12-pounder. There was no wind, so the men manned the sweeps and started rowing as the boats made their way back.

Still smarting the next morning but not wanting to take a total loss, Burns sent some small boats ashore to buy sheep, poultry, and vegetables from local plantations. After gathering provisions, the privateer made haste, putting 20 miles between it and the town, knowing they'd been both unlucky yet fortunate to still be in business with no losses to men or serious damage. Burns wrote he was "going for wool and coming back shorn."

The next day, the *Snap Dragon* captured a British ship headed for St. Croix with cargo and 40–50 "Guinea negroes" or slaves. Eighteen slaves were "very anxious"[17] to go with the Americans instead of continuing to the West Indies, and after taking the merchandise, the ship was released. Another schooner loaded with lumber was captured. Burns had the ship burned, the only time in his career that he destroyed a prize. Records don't indicate why this target was singled out.

The ship sailed to the port of Ponce on the south side of Puerto Rico. The crew needed water and supplies and sold some of the captured goods to pay for it. The Spanish governor on the island entertained Burns, allowed him to resupply, bring on fresh water, and sold him a long nine-pound gun (which was technically a violation of neutrality). The *Snap Dragon* sold some dry goods they'd captured, and the crew stayed in port for several days before heading for the Central American coast known as the Spanish Main.

About five days after leaving Ponce, the *Snap Dragon* chased an English packet, but rough seas ended the pursuit. The choppy waters foretold a severe storm that nearly sent the privateer and his ship to the bottom. Waves were swamping so hard that the guns almost washed overboard and there was three feet of water in the ship. The jibboom was lost. Burns stayed on the deck all night long, fighting the weather and the wheel to keep the ship from foundering and saving all souls on board. His seamanship awed even the most seasoned of sailors, as one crew member said, "She [*Snap Dragon*] wanted watching by such a man as he was, and there was no man on earth that could manage her like him."

Around 4:00 a.m., he felt he had the ship steadied enough that he could go down below deck to rest. However, the wind shifted two to three points and the *Snap Dragon* fell into a trough. The officer in charge didn't recognize the danger until a wave knocked the ship on beam ends and the waist was filled with water—the previously lashed guns afloat on the deck and once again in danger of going overboard. The guns smashed into the bulwarks and damaged the side planks and water gushed in through openings in the ship. Burns quickly made his way back to the deck and, during a lull in the wind, got the guns secured and turned the *Snap* on another tack, which saved it from going down. The captain managed to raise the leak above sea level. He ordered the pumps to start, and it took two hours to clear the three feet of water in the hold. Daylight brought relief from the storm but showed the damage was severe—plank sheer had covered more than 13 feet, so bad "[you] could put in your finger."[18] The storm carried the ship southward.

Burns and the crew headed into a fishing cave near Maracaibo on the Gulf of Venezuela for repairs. He had two talented carpenters on board to manage the job. At that time, Maracaibo was a small harbor of mostly fishermen. Burns got permission from the governor to drop anchor and make repairs and later dined with him. Local fishermen told the crew that several British ships were plying the nearby waters. Within four days, the carpenters had completed their work, and the ship was underway and back on the hunt, spotting five ships. "They soon separated like a covey when a hawk darts in among them," one crew member said.[19] They captured the schooner *Rachael* and two sloops, the *Sisters* and the *William*, which they plundered, releasing two and keeping one as a prize.[20] The prize was loaded with dry goods and dressed skins, and a crew headed with it back to North Carolina.

5. The First Tour of the Snap Dragon

A few days later, the *Snap Dragon* went after another group of three ships under the lee of a fourth, which would turn out to be the British man-of-war HMS *Fawn*. The ship was rigged "in a suspiciously negligent manner, having her fore and mizzen topgallant masts struck while her topsails seemed to be badly patched."[21] The *Snap* took the bait, even though Burns suspected a trap, fired and hit the ship with no response, and discovered that the sails were not patched but had black cloth pinned on to look like patches.

A breeze gave Burns a chance to get away, but some of the officers were annoyed, still not understanding the power of the opposing ship, thinking she was an armed merchantman and upset about the loss of potential prize money. This infuriated Burns and fired up that temper he was now becoming famous for possessing. He told the officers he had as many friends in British prisons as they had and was just as willing to pay them a visit. He promised he'd show them he wasn't wrong, that they were facing a heavily armed British warship: "I hope I can see some of your bravery," he said. Burns set the ship up to lay a broadside into the *Fawn* after a chase that scored a hit. Strong breezes came and went and a squall formed that favored the *Snap Dragon*. Burns furled the topgallant sails and single reefed the mainsail—a move to fold or roll the canvas in on itself to improve performance during sharp winds. He sent all but a skeleton crew needed to work the ship below deck in what one man later called "tight times." Land was ahead, and either way the *Snap Dragon* went would allow the *Fawn* to get closer. The situation appeared so desperate that many men were gathering belongings, as they expected to be captured and sent to a British prison. Just as the ships were about to meet in a moment that would determine supremacy, a breeze fed straight into Burns' sail maneuvers and his ship shot past its opponent at 300 yards. The ships were so close that the men could hear the British officers issuing commands. The British ship tried to change its tack and missed stays but then got on the right track just as Burns changed his tack again. Burns knew his ship well and that it would not miss tacks as it could catch on long ones. But the *Fawn* was one of the fastest ships in British service and had recently sunk an American privateer and was far from done—"The man of war showed his teeth," as one crew member said. The *Fawn* fired a broadside shot of grape and canister, but the *Snap Dragon* was in a fortuitous trough, and the only damage was holes in her sails. Nightfall allowed Burns to escape the close call. One witness on board later wrote, "Nothing saved us that day but the exertions of Captain Burns alone and his skill in sailing maneuvers."[22] Burns told the crew, "Now boys, we are safe."[23]

This is where the first "fake news" emerged. When the *Fawn* made port, it reported that it had sunk the *Snap Dragon* and that Burns' ravaging of the local shipping was over. Burns and his crew found out of their alleged fate when they made port in Curaçao, an island east of Aruba and north of Venezuela. The report wasn't completely unfounded as the conditions were bad, and the hull of the low-lying privateer was barely visible after the British ship had unleashed three broadsides.

Shortly after leaving Curaçao, Burns made his next capture on January 18, 1813: the sloop *Fillis*. A prize crew made it back to Beaufort on February 23.

Off Santa Marta, Burns put the English prisoners ashore at their request but warned them that the Spanish might put them in prison. He sent them ashore with an officer. The men were gone for hours, and when it became late in the afternoon, the officer had not returned. Burns sent another officer with the privateer's commission paperwork and that boat was seized by local officials just as the first had been. After arguing with the Spanish officials, the officer was allowed to return to the ship but without the men. The officer relayed the message that the local officials demanded that Burns anchor the *Snap Dragon* under the fort's guns before the men could be released. Burns didn't trust the Spanish and refused.

By 8:00 p.m., the full moon allowed the Spanish to see every move of the *Snap Dragon*, which was exactly what Burns wanted. The crew raised the sail and headed out to sea as if they were leaving their

5. *The First Tour of the* Snap Dragon

jailed shipmates behind. When the sun came up, the privateer was out of sight. However, the ship was just over the horizon waiting for any ship that left port.

Not long after sunrise, a Spanish felucca set sail and Burns wasted no time in running the ship down. There were 100 men on board and several unmounted cannons intended to fortify nearby Porto Cabello. Burns sent the ship's captain ashore with a message for the Spanish that every man would be hanged unless the *Snap Dragon* crew was released within two hours. Crew members rigged two gallows just to hammer the point home with a visual. As it turned out, the Spanish governor's brother-in-law was among Burns' prisoners. The Spanish complied, and the Americans were released back to their mates. A crew member noted, "There was never a set of men worse frightened than these Spanish, and if that plan had not been adapted, we never would have seen our men again."[24]

Soon after, the *Snap Dragon* headed southwest for Cartagena to replenish the freshwater supply. The privateer ran up on a British merchantman with a 12-gun Spanish brig and an 8-gun schooner providing escort. As Burns got his ship closer, the brig fired a warning shot across his bow. He pulled alongside and demanded an explanation.

The Spanish claimed they were convoying with the cargo ship, to which Burns replied they had no right to do since the United States was at war with England and beyond the neutrality limit of three leagues from land—and they were not in sight of shore. Harsh words followed. He seized the British ship and placed a 21-man prize crew on board and ordered them to stay close to the *Snap Dragon*. Some of the cargo was transferred to the *Snap Dragon*, and the rest was left on board. The prize crew anchored offshore beyond the three-league limit to prevent a Spanish claim. The next day, Burns sailed his ship into port and got permission to refill his water.

One of the Spanish captains landed at a nearby port and sent a message to the Spanish governor at Cartagena that Burns had fired on his ship within the neutrality limits and taken the British prize illegally. Burns was not aware of the false accusation. The governor sent three gunboats to find the prize and opened fire. The crew returned fire. Burns sent five men by boat with instructions to the prize master, but the ship was captured after the Spanish sent two more warships. They captured the prize, arrested the crew, put them in irons, and threw them in prison. The men were also robbed of personal property.

 Burns was furious, but there was little he could do with part of his crew locked up and his ship under the guns of the fort. There was no local U.S. consul or agent—he was on his own. It was clear the Spanish intended to keep the prize, and later it became obvious as to what they were up to. Burns spent the next three weeks negotiating for their release and eventually paid a bribe estimated to be between $15,000 and $20,000. Conditions were so bad that two of his men died in the prison. Once the deal was struck, Burns and his men were delayed another week from leaving port to allow the nearly 20 British ships that were anchored there to escape—they had bribed local officials. In addition, there was more subterfuge going on; while they had the prize ship in custody, the Spanish stripped about $15,000 in cargo and doubloons from a secret cache they'd known about.

 One of Burns' crew members deserted while they were in Cartagena. When he was caught, he claimed to be Spanish. A Spanish captain came on board the *Snap Dragon* to take up an argument about the man with Burns on the ship's deck. Tensions escalated quickly, and a witness described the scene: "Some very high words passed between him and Burns." The Spanish commander drew his sword and Burns grabbed up a boarding pike and was in the act of staving it through the man when he was restrained and the Spaniard left in a hurry. That was the last confrontation in the ordeal. In the end, Burns could not strong-arm his way through the corrupt powers in place. "The whole affair did not cost the stockholders or the Snap Dragon less than $20,000 besides her detention."[25]

 Burns wasn't finished with the Spanish. Shortly after leaving

5. *The First Tour of the* Snap Dragon

port on the way to Jamaica, the *Snap* stopped a Spanish brig and was examining the ship's papers to make sure it was what it claimed to be. Some men on the boarding crew had been among those imprisoned and mistreated in Cartagena, where two of their mates died. While the boarding officer was below checking papers, the crew seized a couple of the Spaniards and quickly started stringing a noose to hang them in retaliation. The boarding officer had to scramble to stop the lynching and talk the men down. He sent them back to the ship. From that point forward, none of the men who were imprisoned were allowed to board Spanish ships.

The *Snap Dragon*'s next stop was Old Providence, 150 miles east of the Mosquito Coast, for supplies as the cruise was nearly at its end. The town had a population of about 700, about three-quarters of which were Black. It was a beautiful place where supplies of cotton, beef, poultry, and hogs could be had at reasonable prices. The port was British property but not garrisoned, so Burns figured that money or force would provide what they needed. When the privateer arrived, they were told they'd just missed a pirate ship loaded with "a large quantity of specie" and whose crew had stolen slaves and cattle from the citizens.

They anchored, not anticipating that another larger-than-life legend from the voyage was about to unfold during what should have been an uneventful day of blowing off steam. Leave was granted for the men to go ashore one-third at the time. The first group went and returned with no problems. The second group found an old lady who ran a "pothouse" or tavern but returned on time and happily shared the location. The last party found the tavern and immediately got ripping drunk. When the appointed time for return came and went, the *Snap Dragon* fired a cannon round as a reminder, which was ignored.

Burns sent an officer and the men of the first group to retrieve their shipmates. The partying crew refused to return, and a sergeant of the marines named Plane, known as a "saucy scoundrel,"[26] told the officer they "had not gotten their frolick out and if the lieutenant interfered with them, they would heave him down the hill."[27]

Captain Otway Burns

Word was sent back to the ship. Burns was furious. He grabbed his sword and had a boat take him to shore, where the brazen Plane was waiting for him.

"Well Captain, when ashore I am as good a man as you are," Plane said.

Burns offered no words but started swinging his sword with determination and accuracy and "cut him [Plane] down, but didn't kill him and attacked the rest of the party, blood everywhere until it ran in streams." Within an hour, all the rebellious men had been subdued, embarrassed, and returned to the ship.[28] A crew member not involved in the melee later said that the men could have overwhelmed the captain and thrown him over a cliff and that he should have taken armed men with him, "but he [Burns] never stopped for anything when he was angry."[29]

They set a course for Cape Antonio on the western coast of Cuba and, for over two weeks, sailed for Havana. They captured a British ship from Honduras, took part of the cargo, and released it, deciding it wasn't worth manning and sending home. The *Snap Dragon* then set sail for Beaufort.

Just north of the Florida Keys off Cape Florida, they fought with the British privateer *Providence* that sported ten guns. The fight carried on until the British ship broke off after losing its long gun and ran into the reefs, with several killed and wounded. The *Providence* eventually made its way to Biscayne Bay, where the heavier-drafting *Snap Dragon* could not go. There was a lot of stress at this point in the cruise as the hold was full with the cargo from a dozen prizes and Burns knew the West Indies waters were "fairly swarming" with British ships and worried more would be stacked all along the American coast. By this point, Burns was a wanted man and the *Snap Dragon* a much-desired target of the British navy.

The next morning, they saw a large-sailed ship and were unsure if it was a British merchant or a cruiser out of Havana. Burns followed it closely for some time. The privateer could not get within gun range until night and did not want to find out in the dark. At

5. The First Tour of the Snap Dragon

daybreak, Burns concluded it was a British ship, showed his colors, and fired a gun to signal the ship to heave to. The ship ignored the message. He got closer and fired muskets, but the ship still would not comply. This is when the Americans discovered the ship had 20 guns and had hands at all quarters—it was a tense confrontation. The captain claimed, in excellent English, to be the *Fernando* going from Havana to Cádiz. Burns checked the ship's papers and decided to release it rather than fight. All involved breathed a sigh of relief.

The next course was for home, to the North Carolina coast. There would be one more confrontation, which proved to be comical in the end. Just miles from home, right off Swansboro, they chased a ship. When they neared the vessel, the crew was pretending to pole even though they were in seven fathoms of water (a fathom is approximately six feet). It turned out the captain was an old friend of Burns and the crews on both ships had a good laugh.

After six months at sea, the *Snap Dragon* pulled into Beaufort in February 1813 with over $1 million in cargo. Burns discharged the crew and put in for repairs. According to the February 27 edition of the *Federal Republic* newspaper, he had delivered several small prizes and the British sloop *Fillis*, apparel, furniture, and 3,000 goat skins. Other reports added 18 slaves, 10 boxes of soap, 6 bales of cotton, leather, cordages, a swivel gun, 5 muskets, 24 cutlasses, 25 pounds of powder, and 200 pounds of indigo in addition to all the booty sent back during the tour. The *Snap Dragon*'s first voyage was a profitable one and set up another mission soon after a refit and recovery.

6

The War Hits Hard

THOSE ON THE NORTH CAROLINA coast and around New Bern, Burns' home port, did not have unfounded fears. Blockades continued to be an issue as the war intensified, and not much in the way of help was coming from the state or federal government.

Desertion occurred at a high rate in 1812, and morale was low among American troops. It got so bad that four months into the war, President Madison issued a pardon to all deserters who returned to their units within four months. Discipline in the service was far ranging and might include paddling, cut in pay or liquor ration, ear cropping, or execution. To increase enlistments, Congress raised the bounty for troops from $40 and 160 acres of land to $124 and 160 acres of land. Privateers got a $100 bounty for POWs.[1] There was a five-year commitment for soldiers at first, then it was extended for the duration of the war. Another adjustment increase moved pay to a $124 bounty and 320 acres of land—possibly the highest military bounty in the world at the time.[2] Privates were paid $5 a month, non-commissioned officers $7–$9, and officers $20–$200. In late 1812, the bottom rate was raised to $8. Men were rarely paid on time, and sometimes the government was as many as 12 months behind schedule. That, along with erratic supply lines and unreliable contractors, took as bad or worse a toll on the troops as the losses on the battlefield.

In August 1812, just as Burns was making plans to get into privateering, the United States suffered its first great land battle loss. General William Hull was bluffed and surrendered his larger force of 2,000 men—nearly one-third of the number of men in the entire

6. The War Hits Hard

army when the war started—at Detroit to British General Isaac Brock and Tecumseh and his warriors. The British held the city for a year and the victory helped boost morale in Canada. It was such a disaster that Hull was court-martialed and sentenced to death by firing squad, but Madison commuted the sentence to discharge from the army because of Hull's service in the revolution and his age—he was 59. Hull was succeeded by General William Henry Harrison. Two months later, Harrison won the first significant American victory at Fort Harrison, Indiana.

There were several defeats on land, but the American navy fared a little better. Many officers saw action in the Quasi-War (1798–1801) and the War with Tripoli (1801–1805). In comparison with the army, the navy was well trained and well supplied, even though privateers provided tough competition because of shorter service commitments, less potential for combat, and higher potential payouts. Boys and landsmen made $6–$20 a month, ordinary seamen $10, able-bodied seaman $12, and gunners $18.[3] The British had a 1,000-ship navy, but it was scattered all over the world and had to supply Spain, Canada, and the West Indies while dealing with Napoleon, who was rebuilding the French fleet.

Even as General Hull was in the Detroit debacle in August, his nephew Isaac Hull was commanding the USS *Constitution* and defeated the HMS *Guerrière* on August 19, 1812. The ship was so damaged that it couldn't be salvaged, so Hull burned it. In October, USS *United States* Captain Stephen Decatur captured the HMS *Macedonian* and sailed it into Newport, the first time a British prize was brought into an American port. The *Wasp* defeated the *Frolic* off the Virginia coast in October, and the *Hornet* took the *Peacock* off British Guinea in February 1813. Captain Henry Lambert was commanding the *Constitution* when it sank the *Java* off the Brazilian coast in December.

However, the most damage on the seas was done by privateers in the first year of the war. In the first six months, privateers took 450 prizes. The British navy was stunned—in 20 years of war in Europe, it had only lost five vessels. They increased ship production.

To encourage more privateering, Congress wanted to lower duties on prizes, but Secretary of the Treasury Albert Gallatin said it would reduce government revenues and not significantly increase privateer numbers. Instead, the government expedited the sale of captured goods, limited some fees, created a pension for wounded privateers, and promoted the destruction of enemy shipping by authorizing a payment of one-half value of the bounty of each vessel destroyed. Duties were reduced to 33 percent, and a $25 bounty was offered for each POW as the United States tried to balance the number of captives taken in the war.

By January 1813, rumors started circulating that some Americans were selling food to the British. The British sold passes for $20 that offered safe and unmolested passage to American ships that wished to sell corn to the Crown. Provincetown, Massachusetts, was openly used by the British. British ships constantly attacked small coastal vessels in Virginia, North Carolina, and South Carolina because of their agricultural cargo. Several merchants in the New England states were accused of dealing with the enemy and some in North Carolina as well, one POW on a British ship claimed. An investigation showed that several important men in Currituck, North Carolina, were involved. The general scheme was that they pretended to have shingles on board their ships headed to Baltimore, but once at sea, they transferred livestock to British ships.[4] The British were blockading south of Massachusetts but not New England, and orders eventually went out to stop all ships headed toward British ships. Some merchants made "dummy" privateers so they could trade, and a brisk business was carried on between the United States and Canada. Down south, the Spanish property of Amelia Island, Florida, was a principal outlet for produce, and there was plenty of smuggling in and out of New Orleans.

To counter this, President Madison proposed an embargo to keep all U.S. ships in port. There was a complete ban placed on goods

6. The War Hits Hard

commonly purchased by the British. There was a ban against foreign ships unless three-quarters of the crew of the ship were citizens of that country, and there was a ban on ransoming ships. The only loophole allowed was for privateers, but the move hurt the economy so badly that Madison asked for a repeal four months later.

The British increased their naval force in North America and extended the blockade northward the same year. Warships and merchantmen started sailing in convoys, which cut down engagements and slowed privateering. The U.S. Navy changed tactics from battle to destroying commerce.

In May 1813, the HMS *Shannon* defeated the *Chesapeake* off the coast of Boston in what is sometimes called the Battle of Boston Harbor. The American crew and captain were inexperienced, and it showed quickly in battle. Captain James Lawrence, previously a hero for his actions on the *Hornet*, was killed but coined the lasting catchphrase, "Don't give up the ship!"

The second year of the war was tougher for privateers. With the change in British tactics, about the only hunting ground left was in the British West Indies or off the British coast, the one area English transports ran without an escort or in convoys. The British were willing to exchange POWs, but as an indication of how effective privateers had been in the early going, they would not consider prisoner exchanges for them. Sailors trapped in Britain were treated poorly in hopes they could be convinced to join the British navy. The British also tried to require that POWs be put on neutral ships or dropped in port and were not subject to exchange in an effort to force privateers to keep them on board, which required time, space, and extra supplies. This was yet another abuse of British sailors committed by their superiors, which was a contributor to impressment to begin with.

There were some American successes as Captain Burns prepared to set sail again. *True-Blooded Yankee* went out for just 37 days in the British Isles and took 27 prizes. It was outfitted by an American living in Paris. *True-Blooded Yankee* occupied an Irish island for

Captain Otway Burns

six days and burned seven ships in a Scottish harbor on the tour. Privateers *Scourge* and *Rattlesnake* combined to take 23 prizes in the North Sea. Other privateers fared well in the area, too:

- *Prince-de-Neufchatel* destroyed $1 million worth of British shipping in one cruise;
- *Governor Tompkins* stripped and burned 14 prizes in the English Channel; and
- *Harpy* returned to the United States after a 20-day cruise, netting $400,000 in cargo.

The British tightened their blockade around Burns' home turf of North Carolina, and calls for help from the federal government came from Wilmington, Beaufort, Edenton, Washington, and Swansboro. The secretary of war finally sent five gunboats to Wilmington. The blockade and shoaling in the channel caused problems for Swansboro's trade and construction, from which the town never completely recovered.

On July 11, 1813, a British fleet under Admiral Sir George Cockburn arrived off Ocracoke with a 74-gun frigate, three smaller frigates, one brig, three schooners, and barges loaded with 2,000 men. Ocracoke and Portsmouth Islands were captured as well as two privateers, the *Anaconda* and the *Atlas*.

The largely undefended North Carolina coast was at risk. The Cape Fear River was threatened by enemy ships and the British considered landing at Beaufort. Taking New Bern was the primary goal. A local customs officer escaped from Ocracoke on a revenue cutter named *Mercury*, outran the British pursuers and made it to New Bern with money and bonds. He warned authorities that the British were planning to move on the city. The invaders looted and destroyed homes and property, taking supplies and livestock from the locals, tore up beds, and took clothing in Ocracoke. They left payment of $1,600, which was about half the value of what they took. Militia companies were called out to march to New Bern and other towns for defense. This prompted the British to leave the area on July 16.

6. The War Hits Hard

In October 1813, the Americans under Major General Harrison defeated the British at the Battle of the Thames, also known as the Battle of Moraviantown, near Thamesville on the Ontario peninsula in Canada. Harrison had more than twice the men of the British and their Indian allies led by Tecumseh. The Americans won quickly and handily, and Tecumseh, along with a number of British troops, were killed. This defeat ended the alliance of the Indians with the British. This was fresh off the September victory by Master Commandant Oliver Hazard Perry, who won the Battle of Lake Erie and eliminated the British presence on that body of water.

That same month, the European war took a turn that would not help the American effort. The allies defeated Napoleon at the Battle of Leipzig in the largest battle in European history until World War I. Napoleon had to withdraw to France in what was the beginning of the end for him, and this allowed the British to divert men and supplies to America. Privateers were also affected, as they had been allowed to use French ports to refit and rearm while Napoleon was in office. Dark days were coming to American shores.

7

The Second Tour of the *Snap Dragon*

Burns' frequent base of New Bern was busy preparing for a British invasion during May and June 1813 as Burns readied for his second tour. There had been attacks and Redcoats had landed at the Outer Banks, occupied an area at Ocracoke Island for a short while, and left, but there was fear they would come farther inland next time. The locals who had opposed the war from the beginning simply wanted it to end.

A second letter of marque had been issued to Burns, and there was a lot to be done before the next cruise of the *Snap Dragon*. Alterations were made to improve the sailing qualities and fighting capabilities of the ship. One important purchase was that of several British uniforms for use in case of emergency. About 75 men were recruited from New Bern and Norfolk, and some reports say the *Snap* piled on 127 men, but that may be a confused number since about 40–50 came from Norfolk, as that would have been overloaded, even with prize masters and crew. There were 5 carriage guns, 50 muskets, and 4 blunderbusses, and a new first lieutenant by the name of James Brown joined the outfit.

When agents for Burns and his partners wrote to New York City for a recommendation for officers, Brown's references offered high opinions of his abilities. Burns welcomed him aboard, gave him instructions, and left Brown in charge with plans to set sail the next morning, June 1, 1813. His first impression was of "a fine-looking fellow and the very looks of him were enough to frighten a common

7. *The Second Tour of the* Snap Dragon

man," as one crew member put it, but later he turned out to be a "bully and a coward."[1] Burns was heading north this time as the military buildup of Canada because of the deepening war effort meant that a steady stream of supply ships would be sailing toward Nova Scotia. He also likely wanted to avoid the summer heat of the West Indies.

Expecting his ship to be ready to sail the next morning, Burns got a most unwelcome surprise. The crew was in "great confusion" and nearly a dozen of his best men were in irons. "One fine old fellow, by the name of Dick, who was a great favorite, looked at Burns as he came over the side and began to cry."[2] Burns sent his steward Jack Parker on deck to have Brown meet him in his cabin. Burns immediately questioned Lieutenant Brown, who replied that the men were "noisy and saucy, and that he would tame the damn rascals and show them how to behave." One man later offered his version that "Dick was cutting some of his monkey capers and the others were laughing at him; that they had just come off from the shore and were 'a little merry.'" Alcohol was likely part of the equation.

Burns informed Brown that this type of discipline might be expected on a military ship, but "that would not do on board a privateer, though perhaps it might do aboard a king's ship," which seems to imply that Brown had once served in the Royal Navy.[3] Apparently, the new lieutenant did not realize that the crew members of a privateer did not work for wages but for shares in the captured prizes. Burns ordered Brown to release the men. Brown said it was beneath his dignity to do it personally and then turned and ordered the master of arms to unshackle them, which riled Burns.

"You put them in and you shall take them out," the captain said, his voice and temper rising. "Now sir, obey my orders or I will run you through."[4] All on board who had sailed with the captain had seen this fire on the first cruise, and Brown had likely heard enough stories to know that these comments were not hyperbole. Brown released the men. By this point, Burns had erased any doubts among the men in his ability as a leader and commander that had come up

Captain Otway Burns

early on the first voyage. The "men idolized their gruff but generous commander."[5]

That night, a boat arrived from Portsmouth, North Carolina, with a message from Lieutenant George Hutchinson of the *Highflyer*, a tender to the ship of the line *San Domingo* that had once been an American ship. Hutchinson wanted a duel with the *Snap Dragon*, just off the shoals of Cape Lookout. Furthermore, Hutchinson added that he was on his way and if the *Snap Dragon* didn't show up, he'd "look into Beaufort"—a clear threat of possible shelling, landing, and/or looting. This was June 3, 1813, just two days after Captain James Lawrence of the *Chesapeake* sailed out to meet the HMS *Shannon*, commanded by Captain Phillip Broke off Boston Harbor. Lawrence was killed, and the *Chesapeake* was captured and put into British service.

Many spectators took to their own boats and made for the cape to see what would surely be a spectacular fight. At eight the next morning, Burns sailed out but only encountered a fellow privateer out of Baltimore, the *Raleigh*. The *Raleigh* went on to Beaufort. The *Snap Dragon* could not find the *Highflyer* around Ocracoke and even sent a boat into the Pamlico Sound to find Hutchinson and his ship, but it was gone. Burns never found the boat that issued the challenge, but about three months later, on September 3, the American frigate *President*, captained by John Rodgers, captured the *Highflyer* off Nantucket.

On June 8, on a course for Newfoundland, Burns ran into a ship off the Grand Bank flying American colors, but the captain was suspicious. Burns had his crew dress in the British uniforms and boarded the ship, which claimed to be the *Neptune* sailing from Wilmington and headed for Cádiz, Spain, loaded with rice and flour. Sailing Master James Smith immediately recognized the captain of the ship as a North Carolinian. The ship's captain pulled out papers and Burns informed him that he was taking the ship as a prize and sending it to Halifax. At this point, the ship's commander produced his "real" papers that offered him protection from British capture. The British issued licenses for U.S. ships bound for Spain which protected them

7. The Second Tour of the *Snap Dragon*

from capture by British ships—Burns had stumbled across Americans who were trading indirectly with the British by shipping goods through neutral Spain. Smith then walked over and shook hands and called the captain by name and the crew of the *Snap Dragon* changed its colors to American. The ship was the *Active* and Burns released it and the cargo (mostly rice), a decision he later regretted, saying he wished he'd burned the traitorous vessel.[6] A witness noted of the *Active* captain, "You never did see any poor devil as frightened as he was. After plaguing him a little while, we let him go, as we had no instructions in regard to licensed vessels. We tore up his license, though. I have heard Burns say since that he was sorry he did not burn the ship."[7]

On June 24, the *Snap Dragon* ran into three British merchantmen off Cape Race, Newfoundland. All three were well armed but shorthanded. After a short action, two submitted by striking their colors, but the third made a run for it. Burns chased the ship for seven hours before the brig finally surrendered. The reason for the daring escape attempt became obvious as soon as the boarding party made its rounds—there was $400,000 in cargo aboard the *Jane*. Burns put prize crews on the *Henrietta*, a bark in ballast out of Liverpool under a Captain Mason, and the *Jane* under a Captain Arkbridge of Martport and sent them to Beaufort. The *Pandora*, a ten-gun brig out of Havre de Grace under Captain Murphy, had no cargo and was released with paroled prisoners. One crew member said the *Jane* "was as fine a brig as I ever saw and her cargo was invoiced at 80,000 pounds sterling." Burns put one of his best prize masters on board. About two weeks later, the crew bore down on what they thought was an American frigate to have a conversation with the captain, but it turned out to be a British ship. The *Jane* was retaken and the crew sent to Dartmoor prison where the prize captain died.

On June 27 at 2:00 p.m., the *Snap Dragon* got within two miles of a sloop when the ship fired a gun and showed English colors. Burns showed American colors and chased even though he thought the ship might be a decoy leading his ship into a trap. He gave chase all night and caught up to the well-manned 12-gun brig in the morning and "engaged in a sharp conflict." Fog settled on both ships, and when it lifted, it revealed nearly 30 ships being convoyed by a ship of the line and several frigates—the outbound British fleet from St. John's headed for England. One of the frigates headed directly for the privateer. The *Snap* crew clapped on sail and held a course parallel to the fleet and "we made two feet to his one," Burns later recorded. But Burns was not fleeing; instead, he boldly worked his way in and out of the cargo ship array, seizing several but ultimately releasing them as Burns did not believe in destroying private property even though he could have burned each of them, the only cargo of note being lumber. A crewman recorded, "We could go in and out amongst the thickest of them in spite of him [the frigate]."[8]

The privateer took a prize that was loaded with dry goods off the coast of St. John's and put a prize crew on board. It never made it back to North Carolina, being captured a few days later.

On June 28, Burns took two more brigs, the *Good Intent* and the *Venus*. He kept the *Good Intent*, but since the *Venus* had no cargo, he loaded the POWs on it and sent it on its way. An armed brig, the *Ringdove*, came after the *Snap Dragon*, but Burns was able to escape and protect his prize, which he stayed with for days before going back on the hunt. The *Good Intent* was recaptured by the British three weeks later.

The next day was a good one. The *Snap Dragon* took out after a ten-gun brig, came up on the lee quarter (the side the wind is blowing on the upper deck), and ordered a ceasefire and for the ship to strike its colors. The ship offered no resistance and complied. It turned out to have $350,000 worth of cargo on board. The commander, Captain Fox, was devastated. He had never been to the United States and expected to be robbed of personal effects, but nothing was taken from him or his crew. He quickly developed a strong friendship with Burns, and as one crew member noted, "he came to love Burns like a brother," and later helped Burns and the men of the *Snap*. Fox's ship was a huge haul, and a prize crew was put on board to head back for

7. The Second Tour of the *Snap Dragon*

Beaufort. Just as the crew was getting aboard, a 16-gun brig sloop, the HMS *Rifleman*, came into view. Burns sent the capture on its way and prepared to engage the British ship to allow his prize to get away. The *Snap Dragon* caught a favorable breeze, but the *Rifleman* was fast. A battle of two skilled captains was underway. One member of the *Snap* crew noted, "For some time it was impossible to say which was the better. Burns said not a word for some time, for he never suffered anyone to talk to him about sailing the *Snap Dragon*." A cat-and-mouse game—with the roles alternating—was beginning.

This went on for more than an hour. Finally, the captain of the *Rifleman* realized after several short shots that he was losing ground on the *Snap Dragon* and went after the prize, which was hull down (partially visible) on the horizon. The *Snap Dragon* then became the pursuer. Strategy and gamble came into play. The British ship had 18-pound short-range guns that could have sunk the privateer easily if it could get in range. The Americans had a long-range 12-pound "Long Tom" on a pivot amidship, and Burns put his best gunners on it and they pounded away at their adversary, wrecking sails, rigging, and masts to the point that the *Rifleman* gave up the chase to go after the *Snap Dragon* once again. Burns shaped a course to draw the ship away from the prize, staying just out of range of the devastating big guns, "teasing" his opponent. The British ship cut the sails on the *Snap*. Once again, the *Rifleman* broke off to make one last run at the prize ship, but the privateer resumed its work with the long-range gun. The prize ship had enough lead to escape as night was coming on, and even with damaged sail, Burns proved to be too good and too fast of a master. By morning, his pursuer and the prize were nowhere in sight.

As it turned out, the prize ship had gotten away. That was the good news, but it was only temporary. Part of the cargo on board the prize was liquor, and the prize crew celebrated its escape by getting drunk and staying that way for days. They were captured 20 days later between Bermuda and Cape Henry.[9] Yet again, the bold Burns' efforts would be lost to the ineptness, drunkenness, or just bad luck.

His boldness and skill resulted in a great number of captures, but the net result was not reflected in the profits.

Burns was furious that his constant success in finding, running down, and capturing loaded enemy ships was yielding no net gain. He took more prizes than any U.S. ship. He gave strict orders to his prize masters to run south and east of Bermuda because from there to Cape Henry was heavy with British cruisers, making it impossible to safely get to Ocracoke or Beaufort. The fate of those captured was the horrendous imprisonment at Dartmoor, where prisoners frequently died. Burns said he was "cursed with a miserable set of prize masters whose impotence, drunkenness or disobedience" caused so many to be recaptured. Every single master who disregarded Burns' advice was caught. Burns could not understand why his recruiters had sent him such incompetent men to perform such an essential duty. Added a crew member, "It was Burns' misfortune always to have a miserable set of masters, and it was strange that the agent and stockholders would go to so great an expense in fitting out a vessel and then ship such trifling fellows for after all, it depends on the prize masters to make a successful cruise."

The next big challenge was a heavy gale off the Grand Bank. The wind was so bad that the crew struck all the yards and topmasts and sent all the guns below decks to add ballast and keep them from rolling around the deck or washing overboard. Burns was on the deck all night until 4:00 a.m. trying to save the ship. The *Snap* was lying to with water breaching over the side constantly. Burns managed to get enough stability to get some relief and go below decks for a short time, but soon the first lieutenant was calling for him—the ship was foundering. When Burns got back on deck, the ship was buried in waves. Burns scudded the ship—running before the storm without the sails set. All the men were distraught and knew the end was near; the ship was sure to sink. One witness said, "She was so very long and so low in the water you might wash your feet out of her stern ports."[10] Suddenly, the situation completely turned, and one man

7. The Second Tour of the Snap Dragon

said, "[He] kept before the wind as the only chance for safety. We had never scudded before, and all hands gave themselves up to be lost. In ten minutes, her waist was clear of water, and I never did see anything skip over the waves as she did in all my life. Still, we knew that the first large sea that struck her, she might go down. In eight hours we were safe, the gale moderated, and we got up our guns and sent up our yards and topmasts. I have often heard Burns say that if a vessel could scud nine knots, no sea could board her; we ran ten knots the whole time we scudded, but I am well convinced that not for his superior management, the sun would never have shone upon us again."

After the storm, the *Snap Dragon* headed for St. John's and captured several coasters, but since they were carrying lumber, which had little value in America, he released them. They spotted what appeared to be an unarmed schooner, but when they got within a mile, aptly named Captain Fox warned that the 14-gun man-of-war HMS *Adonis* was in the area trying to lure privateers with its disguise as a merchantman. It was well armed and crewed.

The ship's topmast was down and the jibboom was drawn in and the sails and rigging were in foul shape. Barrel hoops had been lashed to quarters to conceal the gun ports and no gun could be seen. Burns had been convinced the ship was a coaster, but as they closed, he passed his spyglass to Fox. Fox took a look and said he was more convinced than ever the ship was the *Adonis*. He'd seen her in port at St. John's just ten days before. Fox put his friendship with the American privateer ahead of his allegiance to his country. He told the captain even though he was a prisoner, he did not want to see Burns captured.

Burns took the warning but had waited too late. As the *Snap Dragon* got within 200 yards, the opposing ship's captain decided he could not let the privateer get close enough to board and opened the ports, firing grape and canister broadsides. The *Snap Dragon* returned fire "and a sharp conflict ensued." It looked like a disaster that Burns had taken the bait, and even after surviving the storm, the cruise was about to end. Several men were wounded. Lieutenant Brown, who had started the cruise on the wrong foot by shackling some of the men, left his station and shouted to Burns, "We will all be captured in five minutes. In order to save the lives of the crew, we should surrender at once."

Burns once again flashed his violent temper and Brown felt the wrath—the captain broke his speaking trumpet over the younger man's head and sent him back to his post. A crew member later said, "I wonder he did not shoot him."

Once again, Fox stepped in to help. He told Burns that the *Adonis* had 18-pounders, but they were all short range. Burns returned to the tactics he'd used against the *Rifleman*. While the *Adonis* reset the topmast and jibboom and got her rigging in order, the *Snap Dragon* got out of range and set the Long Tom to work. The *Adonis* was much slower than the *Rifleman*, so Burns literally ran circles around the larger ship and pounded her "very much like a cooper hammering a cask."

Burns then turned the *Snap Dragon* sharply and broke off the fight, using the ship's speed to get away. The *Adonis* chase lasted 28 hours.[11] It was a heavy casualty day for the *Snap*, as four were wounded. This was a more significant number than it might seem because the ship was so shorthanded after having put so many prize crews out. Damage to the ship was mostly to the rigging. Aboard the *Adonis*, three were killed and five wounded.[12] After the fight was over, Burns broke Brown in rank for cowardice and had him sent to the forecastle and station. He made Cokely (or DeCokely) the new first lieutenant.

A few hours later, without firing a shot, they captured an eight-gun brig loaded with salt headed from Liverpool to St. John's and put a prize crew on board. A few days later, in an ironic twist, the *Adonis* recaptured the prize, costing Burns yet again.

Having been at sea a month, the privateer was in need of supplies and worked its way up the Newfoundland coast to Cape Francis

7. The Second Tour of the Snap Dragon

where it came into a fleet of about 90 fishing boats. The *Snap Dragon* ran up the British colors and the officers put on British uniforms. They boarded several ships and traded rum for fish with the fishermen and struck up plenty of conversation. It became apparent to at least one of the fishing boat captains that this was an American ship, not an English one, and he examined the ship carefully. Burns invited the man to his cabin, where the fellow remarked, "Captain, this doesn't look like one of our English vessels, but we don't care so long as she doesn't trouble us." He shared bait with the privateers and the *Snap* crew hauled in over 500 fish on the day.

They dropped anchor at a nearby fishing village and sent the captain of the marines ashore with 25 men to purchase supplies. The men were polite to the townspeople and returned with their ruse intact. The landing party learned a British cruiser was due anytime. As the *Snap Dragon* was leaving, the lookout reported a sail and Burns had all sails put on in case the ship tried to close the entrance to the harbor. The ships approached each other head-on, so it was impossible to determine friend or foe. Burns wasn't taking any chances and tacked as soon as he cleared the harbor and then found the ship to be a three-masted cargo ship. He later learned it was from Bordeaux and loaded with silks, wines, and brandies, headed for Baltimore, an American ship protected with a British license. It was too late for Burns to make a move as the ship had the wind.

After leaving the port, the *Snap Dragon* cruised as far north as 55 degrees 30', close to Cape Farewell in Greenland. This provided another marvel for the crew as they planned to collect rainwater from the icebergs. There was a stream flowing from the top of one iceberg, and the crew sent a boat to land on the iceberg where they found a "lake." They rigged a canvas trough under the stream and filled 20 casks.

The crew learned in Newfoundland that an enormous fleet was expected in from England and would soon be in Canadian waters with ships of the line, frigates, and smaller men-of-war. This hunting would prove to be the richest haul in Burns' career. Not long after

Captain Otway Burns

they cleared the icebergs, the convoy came into view. The privateer tried to stay just out of reach of the escorts while looking for craft to cut out. The *Snap Dragon* was often pursued but outran the pursuers and drew them away from the merchantmen, sometimes returning at night looking for prey.

There was one close call as a fast warship set in on them so near that they had to throw $150,000 worth of goods overboard to lighten the load and take advantage of the *Snap*'s speed to get away. They did it so quickly that the ship became unbalanced because cargo was taken from just one part of the hull, so they had to rearrange. Burns took the boatswain with him and ran up lanyards of rigging and made a few alterations to the sail, and they could see a difference in 15 minutes.

Taking advantage of fog and "teasing" the warships, the crew captured another 10 schooners and 98 POWs over the next several days as the cruise started to wind down.[13] They could have taken more ships, but the manpower was so reduced because of the number of prize crews put aboard captures that they barely had enough men to operate the *Snap Dragon*. Even though there was a bounty issued by the U.S. government for prisoners, on June 24, 1813, Burns had to release them and one ship because he could not accommodate them. They signed a pledge not to bear arms against the United States during the present war until regularly exchanged.

On July 4, the *Snap* captured the schooner *Elizabeth* and used it to resupply. As they headed toward Grates Point, the entrance to Trinity Bay was enveloped in fog. When fog lifted, a frigate pursued. Burns escaped and seized the brig *Happy* and bark *Reprisal* and was after more when the frigate reappeared. Burns released the ships to escape. That afternoon more fog set in, and the *Snap Dragon* ran across and took the *Ann*, a brig headed from Liverpool to St. John's with domestic goods, steel, wire, and crockery—a haul worth at least $400,000. There was so much cargo that it took two days to offload it onto the *Snap Dragon*.[14] Among the listed items were 215 bales of cloth, 22 boxes, 18 trunks, 43 casks, 74 packages, and 22 crates of

7. The Second Tour of the Snap Dragon

earthenware.[15] Lieutenant Brown was put on as prize master of the *Ann*.

They spent the next few days prepping for the return to Beaufort and planning how to get around the British cruisers thick between them and home. They packed the *Snap Dragon* with $150,000 worth of cargo and loaded another brig with the same amount and planned to stick together. The other prizes were ordered to sail separately. They ran up on a British cruiser immediately, and Burns crowded on sail to appear aggressive and it worked, as the enemy ship broke off. The ship was again running low on supplies and was not looking for a fight. Eventually, they parted ways with the prize ship so they could get back to North Carolina as quickly as possible.

On July 22, they spoke with Captain Carinto Sierra of the Spanish ship *Signora Ascension*, which was 96 days out from Lima, Peru. Just two days before, they'd ducked a 74-gun British ship thanks to fog. The rest of the trip was quiet. They sailed into Beaufort and then sweated it out for another ten days before the prize made it in.

The cruise had started on June 3 and lasted 2 months and 21 days and netted property valued between $1.5 and $2.5 million. This was a great success even after all the lost prizes were accounted for—they had taken 29 total prizes.

In the October 2 issue of the *Carolina Federal Republican* in New Bern, Deputy Marshal John Coart ran a notice for "the sale of the brig ANN & CARGO, prize to the private armed Schooner *Snap Dragon*, OTWAY BURNS master; will take place at Newbern on Monday the 11th inst. agreeably to the advertisement of the agents."[16] A sister advertisement from Edward Pasteur and William Shepard, listing them as "agents," advised all creditors and claimants to attend:

> Persons having claims for prize money from the late cruize [sic] of the Snap Dragon, and wishing to purchase GOODS at the intended sale on the credit of those claims, are required to lodge with the agents previous to the day of the sale, the evidences of their demands in order that conflicting claims

may be put in a train for adjustment, and an estimate made of the amount of credit.
EDWARD PASTEUR
WILLIAM SHEPHARD
Agents[17]

The auction was held in New Bern at *Snap Dragon* investor William Shephard's warehouse, and it drew 300 buyers from Boston to Augusta.[18] Some reports say the sale netted $400,000, while another reported $500,000—this may take into account the prize that arrived in port after the *Snap Dragon*. There was an impressive list of items to behold for buyers: "superfine and coarse cloth of all colors and sizes; cassimeres, ditto; gray, brown, and olive coatings; red and white flannels, rose and striped blankets, palms, duffels, kerseys, bombazines, bombazets of all colors, satinetts and rattinetts of all colors; swansdown, striped and figured; prince's, Brunswick and benner cord; flushings of all colors; carpertings, cambric and cambric muslin, cotton shirtings, prints, calicoes, shawls, checkered and fancy molesdown, plain and silk striped toilnenets, Bedford, patent and Windsor cords, velveteens, elastic stockinett, web braces, cotton and silk laces, men's and women's cotton and worsted hose, dimities, love handkerchiefs, beaver gloves, fancy vestulets, sewing silks, boot cord, thread, London and White Chapel needles, 60 casks card wire invoiced at 2,200 pounds sterling, 25 tons of steel and sheet iron; and the contents of 58 packages as yet unknown."[19]

One prisoner, "a fine gentlemanly fellow," claimed that he had $4,000 in personal property that had been seized and Burns not only let him keep it, but he also gave him $1,000 cash to get back to St. John's. Another prisoner named Campbell had helped with the auctions and made a commission. One buyer, a merchant from Baltimore, recorded as "Mr. N—," claimed a package worth $3,000 instead of the one he'd purchased for $1,200 and Campbell refused to give it to him. The irate customer, who was much larger, cursed and then struck Campbell. When Burns found out, he reprimanded the man for abusing a prisoner and then tweaked his nose (a severe pull), "an

7. The Second Tour of the Snap Dragon

insult to which the man meekly submitted." Burns had no more trouble on the auction house floor. A witness said of the merchant, "He was a cowardly scoundrel, for no gentleman would treat a prisoner as so, and that he [Burns] would not see Campbell imposed on."[20]

"'Mr. N—' sneaked off" and found Captain Bates of the *Comet* of Baltimore to complain about his treatment at the hands of Burns. He would get no satisfaction. Bates told the man he had nothing to do with private quarrels and that he and Burns were "on good terms and hoped to continue so." The officers and the crew gave Campbell a barouche (horse-drawn carriage) and a pair of fine horses, and Burns handed the popular man $500. The irony of his haul was not lost on Campbell, who was captured on one of the *Snap Dragon*'s prizes. He told one of the men "if he had gone the voyage safe, he would not have made half as much as he did"[21] working for Burns.

There was plenty of money to go around. The cruise made a fortune for the owners and the crew. The captured *Henrietta* had been sold in September. The only damage during the cruise had come from the *Adonis* and that amounted to no more than sail and line repair. Each crew member walked away with $3,000, an enormous sum for the time and for the length of the cruise—about $52,000 in 2022 currency. The officers received more. At the time of the cruise, a man with $10,000 might be "set for life." Burns got a captain's share and an owner's share. If all the prizes had made it back to port, the payday would have been much larger for all.

The Tories in New Bern and Beaufort who opposed the war and the privateers and didn't want the crews in town welcomed these flush-with-cash customers with open arms. They took them "by the hand and treated with the greatest kindness and invited them into their houses and taverns, only to try to get their money." The fleecing of the sailors was widespread. One tavern in Beaufort made a fortune selling crew members eggnog at a dollar a bowl, some paying with a doubloon and being told it was only a dollar, when they were worth about $8 at the time. Some men tired of waiting for their discharge and payout asked for their prize tickets and one gave Burns

Captain Otway Burns

"impudence." Burns flogged him and had the men thrown in jail. Some local men visited the crew members in jail and offered them half the amount of their prize money, told them they would get their release, and see Burns pay for the flogging. The crew members returned to Burns to get their shares, and he told them they'd forfeited the money and that he'd not pay. They hired a local lawyer named Graham, who advised him to pay but was unaware of the deal and the forfeiture. He met with Burns to read the articles of agreement and realized his men had been conned. They attempted to get the money back, but the sailors had already spent about $200 of the money they'd gotten from the Tories—some of them only got about one-tenth of the value of their shares.

More trouble was brewing. On October 8, just days before the auction, Theodore Skidmore took Burns to court, charging that the captain was "embezzling prize goods [and] cheating profits from the partners of the *Snap Dragon*," according to a letter in the Beaufort courthouse.

On January 13, 1814, Burns appeared in court in Beaufort to answer a similar charge. Besides his legal problems, there was trouble at home. As Burns was preparing for a third cruise, Joanna took Owen and left him to live with relatives in Jones County, North Carolina, roughly 40 miles north of Swansboro and almost 60 miles northeast of Beaufort. Between January 5 and 17, Burns took out two ads in *The Newbernian* newspaper that he was no longer responsible for his wife's debts. Burns didn't linger or mourn the breakup; it was time to go to sea again, both to hurt his country's enemies and to add to his wealth. This internal drive would push him again and again for the rest of his life with positive and negative outcomes.

8

Dustups and Adventures Between Voyages

The *Snap Dragon* was being outfitted for its third cruise when Burns once again returned to Norfolk, Virginia, to recruit crew members. He stayed one night across the border in North Carolina in nearby Elizabeth City at a tavern run by a Mr. Albertson. About 40 people were eating dinner, but since he didn't know anyone, Burns kept to himself. The subject of the *Snap Dragon* came up, and a large loudmouth man got up and said that it was his opinion that the British and Burns had cut a deal or otherwise the privateer could not have captured so many prizes. It seemed like an outrageous claim, but his audience was attentive. The man had no idea Burns was in the room and the captain ignored the talk to a point until he could stand it no more.

"Sir, I have listened to you for some time, and I now pronounce every word you have said about that vessel and her commander to be false; I have commanded her every trip since she has been a private armed vessel and my name is Burns."

The room fell silent and all eyes and ears were on the temperamental Burns. The boisterous man started backtracking and said he was only repeating back what he'd heard. Burns replied he believed the man to be "a Torie and no gentleman." The man left quickly, and the conversation remained polite for the rest of the evening.

The captain returned to Beaufort, and he and his crew were making final preparations, when yet another legendary episode was

Captain Otway Burns

about to begin. About 300 soldiers were in town, mostly militia who tended to get into brawls when they got together, and there was alcohol involved, which was the case most times when they gathered.

It was Christmas Day 1813, and a gale was blowing. The *Snap Dragon* was in Lennoxville (sometimes spelled Lenoxville), a community within the township of Beaufort, with about 20 men ashore and half of the officers. Burns didn't want them mixing with the soldiers and had ordered them not to go to town. A boat from the fort with an officer and four men started from town and, about halfway there, capsized. It was an ebb tide, a north wind was blowing, and it was snowing. Those ashore made no effort to rescue the men, giving them up as lost as the boat drifted toward the breakers. Burns and one of his gunners came up on the scene and asked if no one was going to save the floundering men, and the replies were that the conditions made a rescue impossible and suicidal.

"Will no one go with me?" Burns asked.

All stood silent. The captain and the gunner then went to the wharf and jumped in a boat, lifting as much sail as they thought it could carry. They did not bother to check for oars—a deadly oversight as they wouldn't be able to get back against the wind and tide without being able to paddle.

As the men clinging to the capsized boat neared the point, the four men decided their best chance of survival was to swim while they were closest to land—they did not realize in the howling conditions that a rescue was underway. Two of the men ended up making it to shore, and two drowned. The officer, James Chadwick, had stayed with the boat because he could not swim. Burns and the gunner reached him about 50 yards from the breakers. As luck or providence would have it, as they were hauling Chadwick aboard, the oars from the lost boat came floating by. The three men were two miles from shore, but the boat was good, and they kept close to the wind as they rowed and landed five miles from the fort. Men from the fort ran down and helped secure them. They likely would not have made it if the oars hadn't happened by, and the fort boat was never seen

8. Dustups and Adventures Between Voyages

again. Chadwick was nearly frozen, and Burns and the gunner were soaked and in almost as bad shape. It was evening when they got back to Beaufort.

Just as the exhausted Burns arrived at the boarding house where he was staying, he stumbled into a quarrel between a group of soldiers and some local citizens with more than a dozen men on each side. One of the *Snap Dragon* crew had sided with the citizens and tempers were flaring. Burns worked his way through the parties and spoke only to his man he was trying to pull out of the brewing fight.

One soldier stepped up and cracked Burns in the head with a stick, cutting him all the way to the bone. The stunned privateer grabbed a large black haw stick (a type of club) from a man standing nearby and set into the group of soldiers, knocking three to the ground and wailing away until he broke the stick. Within ten minutes, the fight escalated into an all-out brawl as 50 sailors from different vessels and all the *Snap Dragon* crew that was onshore rushed to the scene, and a vicious fight took place right in front of the boarding house. It started near a woodpile where the clubs were pulled. There were "many broken heads amongst the soldiers," but no sailor was seriously hurt but Burns. At one point, Burns ran up to his room and gathered about 20 boarding pistols he had loaded, intending to put an end to the fight. Several ladies staying at the boarding house intercepted him and convinced him to get his head bandaged, as he was bleeding profusely, before returning to the fight. Crew members got to Burns while he was getting medical attention and prevented him from rejoining the fight. Meanwhile, the sailors turned the tide at the brawl and chased the soldiers all the way back to the barracks.

A dispatch went out that the privateer captain had nearly been killed by the local soldiers, and the officers and sailors armed themselves "with the implements of war" and marched to Beaufort. Among those implements was a field gun they loaded with grape and canister. The men had been issued 12 rifle cartridges apiece. Things had escalated, and tempers boiled over.

At last, Burns realized things were out of hand and sent for the officer in command of the militia. He told the man that all he wanted was for the man who hit him to be punished, "for he was determined to have satisfaction." Eager to avoid bloodshed and a deadly clash, the officer agreed and promised that the man would be disciplined.

Although Burns might have been satisfied, his men were not. He went out to calm them down and told them that for "his sake and their credit, not to do anything that would disgrace themselves and him, that if the soldiers acted like villains, it was no reason they should, he had commanded them on sea and he hoped he could onshore." He told them he'd been promised satisfaction and begged them to return to the ship. They complied.

The soldier was not seen again, and it was said that he ran away the next day. It is not known whether any punishment was applied. He likely made the right choice, as a witness said that "Burns would have shot him sure as day."[1]

9

The Third Tour of the *Snap Dragon*

Even though privateers had a tougher time after the first year of the war, they were still proving to be effective. According to the *Naval Chronicle* in Britain, the hit was substantial: "The depredations committed on our commerce by American ships of war, and privateers, has attained an extent beyond all former precedent." The *Morning Chronicle* added, "On the ocean, and even on our coasts, we have been insulted with impunity." Insurance rates for the Liverpool-to-Halifax run jumped 30 percent for English captains.[1]

Burns and the partners had the *Snap Dragon* ready for its third voyage just after the first of the year, and it left port on January 20, 1814, with 75 crewmen, 6 carriage guns, 75 muskets, 3 blunderbusses, and 40 pistols (at least one other source said Burns had 100 men on the cruise and 2 swivel guns). The crew was headed back to the Caribbean. First Lieutenant Benjamin DeCokely (sometimes listed to as Benjamin D. Coakley) remained in his position. The second lieutenant was James Guthrie and the third lieutenant was Joseph Anthony. Captain Thomas Barker was in command of 14 marines and his sergeant was Alexander Glover. Joseph Myers (sometimes spelled Maires) was the surgeon with John Gardner as his assistant.[2] This voyage was the only one that had a preserved roster. The sailing master was James Smith and the purser was Moses Horne. Moses Griffith, James Cuthbert, Trison Butler, and William Seymour were added as investors.

The ship crossed the bar at Beaufort at 7:00 a.m. and fired a salute to the fort as it headed for South America. Not long after setting out, the crew captured a ship and recorded a written "word of honor" from the prisoners that they wouldn't revolt, then sent them to port with a small crew of men so that the *Snap* could continue on.

Just two days out of port, the *Snap* chased a vessel that struck its colors, but the water was too choppy to board and Burns had to let the sails loose to prevent from capsizing.[3] On January 24, they stopped one ship that turned out to be Swedish, a couple of armed ships, and caught up with a ship that turned out to be American. The drought of good targets continued. Two ships fired on the *Snap* on February 8, but it escaped around the West Indies. Four days later, the crew boarded a Portuguese ship.

The privateer was near the equator by early February, and the heat fouled much of the fresh water on board, a common problem in those days on ships in warm climates. Stories abounded of desperate situations for sailors. In August 1812, the Baltimore privateer *Globe* had exchanged rum for fresh water after things got bleak.

Things were getting tense. Water was rationed, and on February 13, two men were placed in irons for "introducing themselves to a water cask when the ship's company was on an allowance."

Over the next week, they gave chase to a man-of-war before quitting and suffered through a squall. On February 22, short of water, a leak was discovered, so the crew looked to make their way into port for repairs. On February 23, near the island of Maraca off the coast of Brazil, they entered the Arawari River (sometimes listed as Arawan). When the tide went out, they found themselves stuck in the mud about 20 miles upriver. Burns sent a Lieutenant Anthony and some of the crew ashore to get lumber and supplies, which worried the local authorities, who feared a raid. Anthony was wounded on the excursion. They made repairs and floated out with the high tide. While in the river near Point Brown, the *Snap Dragon* was boarded by a canoe of local natives. Attempts to communicate failed, but the ship's crew was presented with a catch of some "elegant fish." Before they departed, Burns shot several macaws and a 15-foot snake

9. The Third Tour of the Snap Dragon

while ashore. They eventually acquired some spars from a smaller ship, the *Saratoga*, before departing.

Off Cape Race, they took two ships without firing a shot and went after a third that tried to escape. After a seven-hour chase, they gave up. The brig and cargo they captured had $40,000 worth of goods, the first big prize of the voyage. They put a prize crew on board and sent the ship home, but it was later recaptured by the British.

On March 3, the *Snap Dragon* was operating off Paramaribo near the mouth of the Surinam River in Dutch Guiana (today known as Suriname). They chased a ship that Burns believed to be a Dutch or British trader, and the fort at Paramaribo fired a gun to signal the would-be prey, an anxiously awaited visitor to the port.

The ship was a large merchant sporting 22 guns and "coppered to the bends" but appeared to have a crew of fewer than 20. Considering that at the time it took five to eight men to operate a cannon, Burns liked his chances. He ran up the U.S. colors and fired a signal for the ship to heave to. The British ship ran up the Union Jack and also fired a shot. Burns tried to maneuver close enough to board so he could use his manpower advantage to take the ship. The opposing captain realized this and took evasive measures with "great skill." This continued from 7:30 until 11:30 a.m. when Burns raised the red flag—which typically meant no quarter would be given or expected—he was close enough for musket fire.

Crew members climbed into the rigging so they'd be ready to jump aboard around 12:20 p.m. The ship opened up from its stern guns and damaged the *Snap Dragon*'s sails and riggings and prevented boarding. For an hour, Burns tried to get in place to board while the crews of both ships exchanged small-arms fire and the British employed grape and canister. It was chaos. One of the *Snap*'s crew members later said, "They beat off our boarders with pistols, cutlasses, boarding spikes, hand spikes and cold shot. When some were swarming on board, they threw stink pots [stone jars filled with explosives], bricks and glass bottles. [The British ship, being much larger, was able to drop the bombs down onto the *Snap Dragon* deck.] We do not know her loss, but suppose she lost considerably, as blood ran out of her lee scuppers."[4] Burns responded by loading his cannon with sail needles and firing into his opponent's open ports.

At 1:30 p.m., the *Snap Dragon* crew again tried to board and put the helm hard up to make a straight course. In an unusual tactic for that time, the British master directed his larger ship for a head-on collision. Burns turned hard to avoid, and the merchant's fore chains tore off his jibboom and bowsprit. A few anxious *Snap Dragon* fighters got on board the British ship, but suddenly a wave carried the two vessels apart, stranding the boarders in a desperate fight. The *Snap Dragon* tried to fight, but with the damage, it fell into the water with a crash and rolled in a trough, unable to do much. The British crew started hauling down its colors—the usual signal of surrender—after being unable to take advantage of the weakened privateer. The merchant ship also had damage and several killed and wounded and the commander realized saving his ship was more important than carrying the fight. They rehoisted the flag and parlayed with the boarders. The choices were to continue with no quarter or to stop the fighting and have the invaders return to their ship. They chose the latter, and while the *Snap*'s crew returned to their ship, the British made sail and got out of sight as quickly as possible.

The *Snap Dragon* crew started clearing wreckage, which was most of the sails, running and standing rigging, the foremast, the main topmast—even the ship's colors had been shot away. They jury-rigged a mast and set the jib and were underway by 4:00 p.m. But Burns was in despair: "Our sails, rigging, and hull is much damaged, and our boat completely ruined." Four had been killed: Boatswain Thomas Green, William Burns, John Hart, and a Black freeman crew member named Charles Morse. Another seven were wounded: William Rogers, Henry Fletcher, Theodore Stickney, Isaac Clark, Malea George, Peter George, and Edward A. Brigden, who lost his right arm. Burns wrote, "Thus ends an action that forces us to run for some post to repair, owing to losing our mast. Had it stood,

9. The Third Tour of the *Snap Dragon*

she was our prize."[5] The men never discovered the name of the British ship.

Three days later, on March 7, the *Snap Dragon* limped into the mouth of the Orinoco River in Venezuela. Third Lieutenant Anthony was sent ashore with men to get timber and supplies. They had to build a raft as every boat had been destroyed in the action. Soon, Burns' experienced crew had bounced back and had a new foremast in place, new spars, and the ship was rigged as a brig. They stayed at anchor for nearly two weeks—long enough that the local authorities came to investigate. Burns assured them he was only interested in making repairs.

The biggest movie-scene adventure of the cruise came when Burns and another privateer captain named Almeda of the *Kemp* out of Baltimore made a joint capture but had a dispute when dividing the proceeds. Things got heated and eventually Burns challenged Almeda to a "yardarm duel," basically a naval take on the customary duel. The two men stationed themselves on the yardarms of their respective vessels and the plan was for the two ships to sail near and around each other while the dueling captains fired muskets, rifles, and pistols at each other. As they set out for open water to settle the score, then ran into a group of merchant ships and captured one each, thus ending the dispute the best way possible in the profession—with more money and no shooting.[6]

Their next action was chasing a ship that turned out to be the USS *Saratoga*. Their last prize came on March 24, an American ship that had been captured by the British ship *Cleopatra* and had a prize crew on board. It had been flying Swedish colors. Burns put Simon Pendleton in charge with Theodore Stickney as the mate to sail the ship back to port. A few days later, they took a ship the British had captured that was full of mahogany, the *Elizabeth*, which turned out to be the only prize of the cruise to make it back to port.

On April 7, the *Snap Dragon* was near home and, once in sight of the Cape Lookout Lighthouse, fired the gun for the pilot and anchored off Shell Castle. They made the Ocracoke Inlet before

Captain Otway Burns

heading up the Neuse River and firing a salute at 11:15 a.m. Two days later, they anchored in New Bern after 79 days at sea. It was the least profitable of the three cruises. By this point in the war, there were fewer merchantmen, more men-of-war, and more competition from other privateers. Still, Burns had captured nearly a dozen ships and cargo valued at over $1 million and added 250 POWs. He'd also done things his way—only burning one ship, when the typical privateer took prize ships and burned those that weren't worth keeping or when sending a prize crew wasn't feasible.

Other well-known North Carolina–based privateers had tough luck after Burns made port. In late April, the *Hawk* was captured, and less than two weeks after that, so was the *Lovely Lass*.

In 20 months, Burns had become a known force on the water, capturing over 40 ships and having at least 25 other encounters that didn't result in prizes. Losses to British shipping were well into the millions. It's been written that Burns accumulated a personal fortune of $4 million. "Otway Burns [was] a terror to all the British in American waters," politician John Hill Wheeler wrote in the 1880s.

Although he didn't know it at the time, it was Burns' last turn as master and commander of the *Snap Dragon*. His marriage had broken up, and he was crippled with rheumatism and other ailments brought on by the conditions of combat and harsh sea conditions as well as the extreme cold and heat he'd experienced. According to a 1916 article by Edgar Stanton Maclay in the Naval Institute *Proceedings*, Burns had taken prizes of $4 million and captured 300 POWs.

Despite Burns being sidelined, the *Snap Dragon* investors pressed on. His ailments—primarily rheumatism—continued to put him out of action, but there were murmurs that his number of close calls had taken a toll on him and he was worried about being killed. Whatever the reasons, Burns was not aboard for the fourth and final cruise. He was also not in Beaufort, which caused part of the confusion about who was in charge.

Captain William R. Graham was put in charge of the ship when

9. The Third Tour of the Snap Dragon

it left port on May 28, 1814, and headed back to the waters around Nova Scotia off Halifax. Some accounts list Lieutenant DeCokley as the commander, and others list Burns, but Graham was the captain. This brings up some interesting questions: Why wasn't DeCokley put in charge, or did he decline to sail without Burns? Did the ship's investors underestimate the value of the seasoned captain, or had they been blinded by earlier success and profits? In hindsight, it certainly appears that the success of the *Snap Dragon* was due to the intangibles that Burns brought to bear.

The *Snap* took a schooner with fish, oil, and beef tongues before its last encounter. At this point, the British had hunters looking for Burns and the *Snap Dragon*. There are reports that the HMS *Leopard* was one such hunter, and it had concealed its guns to make it appear to be an appealing merchantman target. Reports that listed DeCokley as the commander said that he was killed on deck during the battle, which ended on a broadside from the *Leopard*, surrendering only after suffering a mortal wound. English records say it wasn't the *Leopard*. It was the HMS *Martin* that captured the ship on June 30, 1814, and Graham is listed in the POW records. Records at the U.S. National Archives agree Graham was the commander and that not only was Coakley not killed, but he was also not on board the last voyage. The crew members were taken to Melville Island prison, then shipped to Dartmoor until they were exchanged after the war. A watercolor painting of the *Snap Dragon* battling the *Martin* is at the Mariners' Museum in Newport News, Virginia, which is based on that last fateful encounter.

Regardless, reports that Burns had been captured and sent to prison—which appeared in several newspapers—were perhaps wishful thinking. That the British could not bring down Burns is perhaps most colorfully illustrated in *The Newbernian* issue of November 14, 1874: "Like the Frenchman's flea, that he couldn't get his fingers on, so was Burns to the English cruisers detailed to capture him."[7] Historian Lindley S. Butler, in his book, *Pirates, Privateers, and Rebel Raiders of the Carolina Coast*, summed up Burns' abilities:

Captain Otway Burns

"impetuous, recklessly brave, always right in his instinct for action over the more timid counsel of other officers, and uncannily able to see through the ruses used by the British in an effort to decoy the ship into a trap."[8]

Legend says after the capture, the *Snap Dragon* was auctioned at Halifax in July 1814 and sold to a British businessman who got an English letter of marque for an armed merchantman; so in great irony, the ship worked again as a privateer. Captain James Reid, who had once been a privateer on the *Hare*, kept the name *Snap Dragon*. Later, the ship worked as an island trader between Jamaica and Cuba and is believed to have been lost at sea in March 1816.

The year 1814 was a tough one for Burns. He was hurting and out of the action. Joanna died on September 6, 1814, after a "short painful illness." Despite the earlier split and the ad in the paper, many said that it was a "love-filled marriage." It was reported that Burns was sad when he got news of her death. Joanna left Owen with her family for five years before Burns could wrest guardianship. It was a tough time for Owen as well, as he had a hard time adjusting, moving from relative to relative. For Burns, the times of high and lows were just beginning as the end of the war started another series of adventurous chapters in his life.

10

The War Ends

On March 31, 1814, the Allies marched into Paris, and shortly thereafter Napoleon was exiled to the island of Elba, off the coast of Tuscany, Italy. Suddenly, fear struck the American people. They were no longer fighting for better treatment and rights in trade and at sea or to gain land in the form of Canada. Now, depending on Britain's willingness to continue its wars, America was fighting for its existence. There were people that worried the young nation would fall back under the Crown or lose vast swaths of territory.

The British had plundered the Chesapeake area in 1813 and were threatening to return. A controversial former American naval commander and privateer devised a plan to delay the enemy. Baltimore-native Joshua Barney signed onto a Chesapeake Bay pilot boat when he was 12 years old and at 15 became captain of a merchantman when the captain, his brother-in-law, died at sea.[1] In the Revolutionary War, he was commissioned as a lieutenant and served with distinction on various ships. In 1794, when American ships were being harassed by the British, French, and Algerians, the United States finally commissioned warships be built to address the situation. Dissatisfied that he was ranked fourth instead of third in seniority, Barney declined his commission for one of the new ships.[2]

He secured a commodore's commission in the French navy in 1796 and fought the British, which was not a problem until the Quasi-War broke out with France in 1798. While he refused to attack American ships, some referred to Barney as a "pirate and traitor" and some in the media compared him to Benedict Arnold.[3] Barney resigned from the French navy and returned to America in 1802, working as a merchantman, where he managed to reclaim his standing and shake the disloyal reputation in Baltimore. When war broke out with the British, Barney quickly lined up investors and received the first letter of marque of the conflict. His ship, the *Rossie*, had 12 guns and captured 18 prizes along the East Coast.

In 1813, British Rear Admiral Sir George Cockburn waged war on the tidewater areas of Virginia and Maryland, taking on privateers, commandeering local provisions, burning buildings, and skirmishing with local militias. Barney wrote a letter to Secretary of the Navy William Jones outlining a plan to use small boats to harass and delay the British navy and to keep them away from Baltimore and Washington, D.C. Jones liked the plan and thought Barney was well suited to it, but service politics prevented Barney from being able to be commissioned at the proper rank. Jones came up with a solution: he made Barney acting commandant of the newly formed Flotilla Services, a branch outside the regular navy that reported to President Madison. Barney was made captain. Barney put the flotilla into action in May 1814; it became known as "Barney's Flying Squadron" and also "the Mosquito Fleet"[4] because of the ships' small size, maneuverability, and speed.

Barney was successful until he eventually drew enough British attention that his ships were bottled up in the Patuxent River. He fought and harassed the enemy until August 16, when he could no longer avoid entrapment. He scuttled his ships to keep them out of British hands, and he and the crew members moved overland to link up with Secretary Jones and General William H. Winder to help defend Washington. They ended fighting in the Battle of Bladensburg (Maryland), and after four hours of hand-to-hand combat, which included Barney being shot in the thigh, their position was overrun and Barney was captured. Barney's men were among the last remaining, as most of the American forces fled in a chaotic retreat that became known as the "Bladensburg Races." Winder ended up being court-martialed as a result but was acquitted. Because of his wounds, Barney was paroled and went home (he died in 1818, believed to be

10. The War Ends

from complications from the bullet that could not be removed). The British continued their advance on the capital.

The low point of the war arrived a week later on August 23–24, 1814, when the British burned Washington, D.C., and Dolley Madison made her brave rescue of several important artifacts, including Gilbert Stuart's iconic Landsdowne portrait of George Washington. She left her personal belongings behind and could not get enough transportation organized to save White House records. The city was poorly defended and disgraced and now seemed in its most serious peril. The British took souvenirs, then set fire to the Capitol, the Library of Congress, the Treasury, and the building that housed the Departments of War and State. The shipyard, two ships, and the offices of the *National Intelligencer* newspaper were burned. The Patent Office was spared when English-born Dr. William Thornton, the superintendent, convinced the British that the office contained private property and "models of the arts ... useful to all mankind."[5] The fires burned all night, only to be extinguished the next day by storms, which also blew down several damaged buildings. The burning of Washington was not only criticized in America but also across most of Europe. On August 25, the British left. The Madisons returned to the city on August 27.

In early September, the British again set their sights on Baltimore, which was a key commercial center and a base for several successful privateers. As the British marched through Upper Marlboro, Maryland, the outlook was bleak, but an inspiring story and the young nation's national anthem would emerge. As troops came through the town, a couple of drunk stragglers raised a ruckus. This upset one of the town's leaders, Dr. William Beanes, so much that he made a citizen's arrest and locked the men up. One man escaped and literally came back with an army. They promptly took Beanes into custody on board a ship in Chesapeake Bay.

Ironically, Beanes had been an opponent of the war and had welcomed the British troops to town initially. Beanes needed a lawyer,

Captain Otway Burns

so he called on his friend Francis Scott Key, who came out to the ship to negotiate his release. While on board an American ship tethered to a British ship, the shelling of Fort McHenry began and the men were not allowed to leave. Key was inspired to compose what would become the "Star-Spangled Banner," which several years later became the national anthem. Key had also used the same tune years earlier in a song to honor Stephen Decatur, Jr., and Charles Stewart for their heroics in the Tripoli War.

It was a dark time for Americans. About 13 percent of U.S. troops deserted, almost half of them having been recruited in 1814. Desertion was supposed to carry a death sentence, but to get men to return to the ranks, a ruling was made to pardon the first offense of deserters and only carry out executions for second-time offenders. The government was in financial duress with rising operational expenses and perpetually behind 6–12 months on pay for the men. In November, the government defaulted on the national debt. A lot of trade continued to flow to Canada, which helped keep the British forces supplied.

Negotiations for peace started in August 1814 in Ghent, Belgium, which Madison had been pushing for since March 1813. The U.S. negotiation team consisted of Jonathan Russell (minister to Sweden), John Quincy Adams, Albert Gallatin, Henry Clay, and James Bayard. They waited six weeks for the British team to arrive.

Peace talks were not going well, as the British insisted that Indian reservations be established for their allies in the northwest, and they demanded territory in Maine and Minnesota as well as demilitarization of the Great Lakes and no commercial fishing in Canadian waters. Once again, regional divides were apparent—the middle and Southern states opposed these terms, while the Northeast did not. The British were in no hurry, as they felt the war was going their way and that a few more won battles would force their demands to be met. The delay actually worked against the British as Great Britain, Austria, Prussia, and Russia were trying to sort out

10. The War Ends

the spoils of defeating Napoleon, which included territory in Europe and French, Dutch, and Danish colonies. Essentially, European borders were being completely redrawn. Poland and Saxony were major issues.

Madison was often sick during this time, which curbed his influence. Politicians did not want to let a good crisis go to waste, and many tried to use the destruction of Washington as the opportunity to move the nation's capital back to Philadelphia, while others wanted to put it in New York. Such maneuvers were defeated in Congress. Because the Library of Congress burned, Thomas Jefferson's 10,000-volume library, appraised at nearly $24,000, was purchased. Military challenges continued to mount—the secretary of war estimated that 100,000 men were needed to conduct the war, while only 30,000 were in service.[6]

There were internal problems, much like Revolutionary War times. The Hartford Convention, held by the New England states from December 15, 1814, through January 5, 1815, was one long rant and a potential threat of secession, particularly if the war dragged on. The delegates came up with several changes they wanted to see:

- A two-thirds vote of Congress to declare war, interdict trade with other countries, and admit states
- A 60-day limit on embargoes
- An end to the three-fifths counting of slaves for congressional representation
- A ban on naturalized citizens holding federal office
- Term limits of one term for the president and a provision to prevent electing a president from the same state twice in succession

With all the defeats on the battlefield, the disaster in Washington, and the internal strife, things were going quite differently at the peace talks in Belgium that would eventually produce the Treaty of Ghent. "It was here ... that the United States consistently outmaneuvered the enemy, and it was here that Americans could claim their most significant victory." It was not because of what the American envoys won; it was what they avoided losing.[7]

Peace negotiations started almost from the day war was declared, evidence that neither side wanted a fight. Right after war was declared, the British repealed the Orders in Council. Britain thought this would end the war and was why they waited until October 1812 to begin its military campaign. The United States sent three peace commissioners: Albert Gallatin, John Quincy Adams, and James A. Bayard. The British rejected an offer by Russia to conduct peace talks. America eventually added Henry Clay and Jonathan Clay to the team.

After some success and the ending of the war with France in mid–1814, the British got hungry eyes for what they could acquire in a peace settlement. They wanted at least part of Maine, as it was a barrier between Halifax and Quebec (they occupied Maine until April 1815). They also wanted navigation rights on the Mississippi River and for the United States to completely disarm itself on the Great Lakes.[8] They also wanted an Indian buffer state carved out of Ohio, Indiana, and what would end up being most of Illinois, Wisconsin, and Michigan—an area bigger than England, Scotland, Wales, and Ireland combined—that would be under British guaranty forever.[9] They dropped that demand in September but in October presented a note to the American team questioning the legality of the Louisiana Purchase. By October 18, the United States rejected these terms and offered its "status quo" proposal—a return to the borders and relations in place before hostilities began.

The Gulf Coast campaign was another story in an otherwise bleak tale. That part of the young country didn't have many citizens and was lightly defended. New Orleans was the largest city west of the Appalachians and a major trading hub. There were numerous potential American allies in the area—Indians, Spanish, French, and the free Black population.

General Andrew Jackson wanted to take Pensacola, but politicians

10. The War Ends

in Washington feared drawing Spain into the war. Jackson thought the British would attack Mobile, so he raced to New Orleans and arrived on December 1, 1814. Jackson thought the city could be defended and went to work energizing the different groups and alliances that he could leverage. Louisiana militia Captain Louis D'Aquin brought a battalion of Haitian refugees commanded by Captain Josephy Sarvary, a free Black man who had served in the French army. Jackson also had slaves enlisted who were promised freedom after the war if they served in his army. A group of Baratarian pirates offered their services to Jackson after the British tried to recruit them to attack the Americans. Legendary pirate/privateer/smuggler and leader of the Baratarians Jean Lafitte got along famously with Jackson and joined the defenses. After the war, at the request of the Louisiana Legislature, the pirates were pardoned because of their service. Lafitte was no saint, though, and went back to work as a pirate/privateer and even spied for Spain after the war.

The British assembled a 10,000-man invasion force in Jamaica under General Edward Pakenham, brother-in-law of the Duke of Wellington. He tried to recruit Indians in the New Orleans area by offering to return land to them off the Florida coast, but he got little response. Jackson wanted to attack outside the city before the British could amass full strength. On January 8—later glorified by country singer Johnny Horton's take ("The Battle of New Orleans") on an old tune called "Jackson's Victory"—the main attack took place. It was the most lopsided battle of the war and actually took place after a peace agreement had been reached by negotiators in Europe. Pakenham was killed, and the British lost 2,000 men, including 500 men taken prisoner. American forces lost 70.

Peace had already been agreed to on Christmas Eve, and what an odd treaty it turned out to be. The key issues ended up being fixed boundaries, the navigation rights of the Mississippi River, the disarmament of the Great Lakes, and fishing rights.[10] In the final document, there was no mention of the maritime issues that caused the war, and it essentially returned both sides to the status quo. There was no official settlement of British impressment, but it stopped. It is estimated that 2,410 sailors had been impressed up until 1803, 6,057 from 1803 to 1810, and that a grand total of around 15,000 was the final number. Federalists said that this number was greatly exaggerated.[11] In the end, "the disagreements that started the war and sustained it were acknowledged by both parties to no longer be important"—impressment and maritime rights.[12]

Prizes taken off the American coast within 12 days and distant areas within 120 days of the treaty had to be returned. Peace was made with the Indians, and the border between the United States and Canada was fixed. Native Americans could no longer count on British intervention or help in maintaining a buffer with white settlers.

The War of 1812 is often called America's Second War of Independence, as the country once again stood up to the mighty British Empire. This time, the French proved to be great allies, only indirectly—the British had to focus their efforts on the war in Europe for most of the conflict, and once France was defeated, the infringements on U.S. rights ceased. Major changes in the collective American psyche were put on track and things would forever change on the continent. The purchase of Florida from Spain at almost no cost happened before the decade closed, and the way was paved for the Monroe Doctrine in 1823 and Manifest Destiny. It was the last time America would be the underdog in a war.

11

Postwar Ventures

BURNS WAS NOW A RICH MAN and retired from working as a captain. His adventures and successes had exacted a price in his health and personal life. Regardless of what his feelings might have been about his ex-wife or how sad he might have been—as was reported by many close to him—he did not mourn his failed marriage or Joanna's passing for long. She left him in January 1814 while Otway was on the last cruise, and she died in September. On December 4, Burns married 18-year-old Jane Hall of Beaufort. He had turned 40 that summer.

Life, while good, was not without conflict. Owen did not get along with Jane and reportedly did not speak to her once he became an adult.[1] Burns soon left Swansboro and Onslow County and headed to neighboring Carteret County to make his way in postwar life. Carteret was one of the original North Carolina counties, named after lord proprietor Sir George Carteret, a knight and baronet who died in 1695. Carteret was succeeded by his son John, who was later the Earl of Granville. Granville County in North Carolina is named after him. Carteret County is bound to the north by the Pamlico Sound and Craven County, to the south and east by the Atlantic Ocean, and to the west by Onslow and Jones Counties.

The following April, Burns and his bride bought a lot on Front Street in Beaufort, the county seat of Carteret. They built a house between Pollock and Marsh Streets where they'd live for 20 years and where the fabled Atlantic Hotel would later be built in 1854. Burns also owned and operated a 340-acre plantation on the North River in Carteret County, where he owned 11 slaves.

Captain Otway Burns

The home Otway and Jane built was "a handsome residence" on Lot 16, Old Town, which started 132 feet east of Turner, north of Front, ran 66 feet east and 330 feet north (in the vicinity of the current Cape Lookout Seashore office and some of the Beaufort Historical Association property).[2] He owned a store on an adjoining property that he leased on Front Street "as early as 1819 and as late as 1829."[3]

The area around Beaufort was formerly home to the Machapunga and Coree Indians, who fought each other and battled in the Tuscarora Wars almost to the extinction of both tribes. Settlers arrived in 1709, making Beaufort the third oldest town in the state behind Bath and New Bern. It was first known as Fish Town and later renamed for Henry Somerset, the Duke of Beaufort, in 1713, the same year Governor Thomas Pollock started a garrison and the Core Banks and Core Sound (that were named after the Coree Indians). John Porter received a grant for 7,000 acres of Outer Banks land from Drum Inlet to what was known as Topsail or Old Topsail Inlet. The 1720s saw an influx of immigrants from New England, fishermen and whalers, and in 1722, the Lords Proprietors established a port. The grant was acquired in 1723 by two brothers-in-law, John Shackleford and Enoch Ward—for whom Shackleford Banks and Ward's Creek are named. Shackleford took the western portion and Ward the eastern. The town was incorporated in 1723 at 200 acres, up from the original 10 acres, that was laid out on the property of Robert Turner in 1713.[4] It was known for fishing, whaling, lumber, naval stores, shipbuilding, and farming and had been a port of safety since the late 1600s, largely because of its stable inlet. It was the safest and most navigable harbor of any North Carolina port but almost completely isolated from the state's interior. However, by 1725, a road had been built from Beaufort to New Bern.

The area became immortalized in pirate lore as it was one of Edward Teach's (aka Edward Thatch, aka Blackbeard) favorite haunts. After a two-year run of success, Blackbeard started working

11. Postwar Ventures

the North Carolina Outer Banks. He ran his ship, the *Queen Anne's Revenge*, aground just offshore in 1718 as part of a plot to end to his relationship with another well-known pirate, Stede Bonnet, marooning some of his own men. Blackbeard used the ship *Adventure* after that.

Beaufort quickly became the third largest port behind Port Roanoke and Port Brunswick, moving naval stores, lumber, provisions, whale oil and bone, leather, and livestock. Shipbuilding grew in the area during the revolution, and in the early 1800s, the fishing industry for mullet before the Civil War and menhaden after the war grew. In 1804, Congress set aside money for a lighthouse at Cape Lookout, which was put into service in 1812 and later replaced with the current lighthouse in 1857–59. That same decade, nearby Morehead City became a rival port and today is one of the state's two currently active ports, along with Wilmington. In the last two years of the Civil War, Admiral David Porter used the port as a staging area for the fleet that would take Fort Fisher in Wilmington. This was the area that Burns set out to grow his fortune in his second career as a businessman.

The captain used his newfound wealth to set up shipbuilding operations in Swansboro and the booming town of Beaufort and invested in several local businesses. Burns used a specific wood from the region near Shackleford and the Core Banks and quickly established an excellent reputation for his craft. He employed 11 slaves in his shipbuilding and other business interests. He and fellow shipbuilder Elijah Pigott—whose shipyard had outfitted the *Snap Dragon*—had a setback in September 1815 when two ships on stocks at the Pigott and Burns Shipyard were destroyed by a hurricane.[5]

Steam navigation arrived on North Carolina waterways in 1818 when the *Norfolk* arrived to run between New Bern and Elizabeth City. It would not last, though. The legislature eventually chartered 27 steam navigation companies between 1817 and 1861. It was a struggle because North Carolina lacked "competent ironworks."[6] The former privateer made history in 1818 when he built the first

Captain Otway Burns

Sketch of the *Prometheus* from James Sprunt's *Tales and Traditions of the Lower Cape Fear, 1661–1896*, Wilmington, North Carolina, 1896.

steamship constructed in North Carolina, the *Prometheus*, at his shipyard in Swansboro near the mouth of the White Oak River. The machines and engines were fabricated in Boston and then shipped to Swansboro to be assembled.[7] In the Governor's Letter Books 19 and 20, there is correspondence between North Carolina Governor William Hawkins and steamboat inventor Robert Fulton. In a letter dated December 9, 1813, it's indicated that an associate of Fulton's was due to visit North Carolina to inspect the coast in the area of the Neuse River and make recommendations for improving intrastate navigation, water transportation, and commerce.[8] It is unknown whether Fulton or any of his partners visited with Burns or any other potential builders. He was in a race with builders in Fayetteville who were building the *Henrietta*, and there was a lot of press coverage. This brought out the well-established, competitive nature of Captain

11. Postwar Ventures

Model of the *Prometheus* by Jim Goodwin (courtesy Jim Goodwin).

Burns. Financing was by a joint stock company in Wilmington. It operated on the Cape Fear River between Wilmington and Smithville, which later became known as Southport.

The *Prometheus* was the first to operate on the Cape Fear and was built for Captain James Seawell and Associates. There may have been other owners, as connections to the Clarendon Steamboat Company have been found and D.K. Dodge ran an advertisement in a local paper for claimants to present bills for payment related to the expenses of the steamboat.[9] Although some reports said Captain Thomas N. Gauthier went to get the ship, it was Burns who delivered the *Prometheus*.

The ship was launched on May 6, 1818, but didn't leave for Wilmington until June 1, as it was delayed by heavy gales. There were passengers and cargo on board. Burns navigated south through Frying Pan Shoals and into the mouth of the Cape Fear River. Some reports said he "fought a receding tide," which might have indicated a lack of power.[10] The vessel reached Wilmington on June 10. Burns said that people in Wilmington were swarming the docks, ringing bells, waving, and firing cannon in creating a spectacle. Ever the showman, Burns was on the deck in full uniform. As he rounded the Dram Tree, a well-known navigational marker, Burns was heard to yell into his speaking trumpet, "Give it to her, Snyder!" a command to engineer John Snyder. For years, this became a catchphrase in the Wilmington area and was said to be heard shouted in many local tavern celebrations that night. The *Prometheus* started operating regularly on June 15 with a $1 fare for passengers each way. Other steamers arrived soon, and the rival *Henrietta* was active just a few days later.

The *Prometheus* was over 100 feet in length and had a 15-foot beam and large paddle wheel.[11] When President James Monroe visited the area in April 1819, he rode the ship to inspect Fort Johnson with Secretary of War John C. Calhoun.[12] The *Prometheus* had a "checkered career" after that highlight.[13] It went out of service in 1825, most commonly believed because of a lack of power and because steamboat improvements had made the ship no longer competitive. One account says that the ship accidentally burned at a wharf and was abandoned that year.[14] Today, a historical marker notes the location of the first launch near the town of Swansboro.

Later that same year, 1818, Burns ran a notice in the *Newbern Sentinel* to sell "his dwelling house in the town of Beaufort, and the storehouse adjoining, with a good kitchen, smokehouse, and stable. The stand, for business, is equal to any in the place. Also, four unoccupied lots in said town, and a small tract of land on North River." Burns offered a "liberal credit" and "notes negotiable at either of the banks in Newbern." Burns must have been feeling some kind of financial pressure at that point, as he ran another notice in the *Sentinel* on October 10, asking that all those who owed him money to please pay up "as he intends shortly to remove out of the state."[15] There are no records and no correspondence as to what Burns was considering, although it could have been a ploy to collect debts. He continued to invest in the area, borrowing heavily to the point of being overextended. Within a few years, he committed to politics by running for the state legislature.

11. Postwar Ventures

Burns also continued to watch the waters. In September 1819, the *Santa Maria*, captained by Joaquim Jose Vasquez, was "met on the high seas by an armed cruiser called the *Irresistible*, and was forcibly and piratically captured and seized" off the coast. The *Irresistible* crew tried to bring the *Santa Maria* and its cargo to port but grounded it on a bar in Beaufort Inlet. Burns wasted no time in gathering his own crew to salvage what he could of the cargo, a common practice. Attorneys for Vasquez sued Burns, and county register J. Brown issued a statement in the September 18 and 25 editions of the *Newbern Sentinel* urging all those concerned to show up in court in New Bern in October were "authorized, empowered and strictly enjoined ... to cite and admonish said Otway Burns and all persons having or pretending to have, any right, title, interest or claim, in or to the said materials and cargo of the ship *Santa Maria*." The case was set for Pamptico District Court, with Judge Henry Potter presiding.[16] Vasquez disputed his ship was in peril after grounding off Beaufort following the pirate attack and Burns was taking advantage of maritime law to claim a portion of the proceeds from an auction of the cargo after rescuing it—the question was if the ship was in danger of sinking or just stranded. An agreement was eventually reached as the *Santa Maria* cargo was auctioned. Early in January, Burns was involved in a salvage libel case over the brig *Don João Sixto* as well.

Also in 1819, Burns sold the Swansboro shipyard to William Pugh Ferrand, one of the area's chief exporters of naval stores, the postmaster, and one of the area's wealthiest businessmen. Included in the sale was a lot where Ferrand would later build a structure known as the Olde Brick Store in 1839. The lot, which had a store on it, sold for $400. (The structure still stands today and is sometimes known as the Ferrand House and is in the National Register of Historic Places.) It's possible Burns built another ship, the brig *Rambler*, but eventually closed his shipyard in 1842 due to lack of business.[17]

Burns owned a store that sold supplies and fishing equipment, and operated a taproom from his Beaufort property. In 1820, he partnered with Asa King to buy ten acres on Taylor's Creek and built a saltworks, where they boiled ocean water. The two were partners for at least six years, recruiting and training workers.[18] Burns may have been involved later, but it was mortgaged in 1826.[19]

Burns owned a handful of fishing boats, including a mullet boat, a schooner (the *Venus*), a flat (the *Elizabeth*), a sailboat, and even a canoe. Burns still sailed and maintained his competitive, aggressive edge, replying on at least one occasion to a challenge to show that he had not lost his mastery of sail or his ability to raise the stakes of a situation. The January 4, 1823, edition of the *Newbern Sentinel* featured a notice from Burns that he had accepted a bet on a race:

> Challenge Accepted
>
> The owners of the "unequalled, fast sailing Pleasure Boat DANDY," are informed, that I accept their challenge, "to sail from Newbern to Johnston's Point and back, for Two Hundred Dollars"—and am willing to extend the bet to One Thousand Dollars. My boat is eight inches shorter than the Dandy; and, although the challenged party is generally permitted to name the time, I am willing to waive that privilege, and request the challengers to inform me what day they propose for the race, that my boat may be in readiness.
>
> OTWAY BURNS,
> Beaufort, December 26, 1822[20]

Burns also had an interest in a brick-making operation. Later, he'd produce bricks for the construction of Fort Macon and become embroiled in a controversy there as well.

Burns entered many ventures to make money, but it seemed he always found many ways to lose it. One of his biggest problems was loaning money or investing in the businesses of friends, only to have them be slow in paying or not pay at all during tough economic times. He started feeling the pinch while he was in office.

In 1823, his chief backer and longtime friend, Pasteur, retired from his medical practice. Pasteur was wealthy and moved in high social circles in New Bern. The *Raleigh Register* reported he passed away later that year from an inflammation of the bladder. The *Carolina Sentinel* of New Bern said, "He died at his seat in the vicinity of

11. Postwar Ventures

this town after an illness of a few days.... Colonel Pasteur joined his country in her struggle for liberty and was the ever zealous advocate for the principles of the Revolution. In the various relations of private life—husband, father, friend—he was kind and affectionate. Of his benevolence and liberality, the many whose wants he relieved can bear ample testimony."[21] He was 63.

It was a big loss for Burns, as Pasteur was not just a business partner and frequent financial backer but also a loyal, longtime friend and political backer. He was also Burns' primary connection to the wealthy upper class in Carteret County society. Pasteur was "one of them," while despite his successes, Burns was not.

Despite returning to land and hanging up his cutlass, Burns had many battles back home in his private life, a mix of huge successes and just as huge defeats.

In 1823, he built the *Warrior* in his shipyard, the last of his large boats.

There was plenty of controversy to be had and some adventures as well. Burns continued to add to his legend with a series of exploits in the local North Carolina coastal waters.

On June 3, 1825, a hurricane rolled in during the early hours of the evening and raged until five o'clock the next morning. It rocked the East Coast from Florida to New York, driving 25 vessels ashore at Ocracoke, 27 at Washington, and several in New Bern, which suffered severe waterfront damage. Plantations in the area flooded, and the tide rose six feet at New Bern.[22] The water in Beaufort harbor rose nearly four feet above normal, and ships were overturned and driven from where they were anchored. Trees were down in the town's streets, pulled up by the roots, and several injuries among the citizens were reported, and there was substantial property damage near the wharves. The storm raged up and down the East Coast. It was reported that so much water was blown out of the Potomac River that steamboats had to stop running for fear of being grounded, and a number of wrecks were reported around Baltimore, Philadelphia, and New York.

Captain Otway Burns

The *Argo*, a 200-ton brig out of New York, ran aground on the shoals of Cape Lookout, 12 miles from shore, after the powerful storm of "wind and rain commenced, and continued with great violence until 5 o'clock in the morning. The water in the harbor rose nearly four feet above its usual height."[23] The ship was 12 days departed from New Orleans. A sloop, the *Leopard* (one source lists the ship as the *Leopold*), from Bridgeport, Connecticut, captained by George L. Hart of New York and headed for Wilmington, approached the ship, looked it over, and sailed on. Burns gathered a crew and set out for the shoal. They boarded the *Argo* and found "she had bilged, was water-logged, her mainmast and rudder gone, the sea making a breach over her."

It was an eerie scene—there wasn't a soul on board the *Argo*. However, there were several opened trunks on the deck and articles of female clothing tossed here and there. Burns and his crew concluded that the crew and passengers had picked whatever they could wear and escaped. The ship was loaded with cotton, tobacco, and pork. Seeing Burns and his crew on board the *Argo*, Hart returned to the scene. Working together, Burns and Hart towed the stranded ship to the Beaufort bar, also known as Old Topsail, but its draught grounded the *Argo* once again. The two captains got 200 bales of cotton, 350 barrels of pork, and 90 hhd (hogsheads, which was about 63 gallons) of tobacco offloaded and safely in port.[24] A notice in the *Fayetteville Weekly Observer* on June 23, 1825, announced an interlocutory decree of the District Court of the United States for District of Pamptico[25] providing for a public auction on July 11 for the cargo of the *Argo*. Captain Ellikson is listed as the commander of the doomed ship, and in addition to the pork, tobacco, and cotton, other items are mentioned such as rigging and furniture and 45 or 50 hogsheads of tobacco (about half as much tobacco as earlier reported). The notice was placed by Marshal Beverly Daniel and noted as "Libelled for Salvage, by George L. Hart and Otway Burns, on behalf of themselves and all others entitled."[26] Libeled for salvage is a term that means any person who helps recover the cargo of a ship in peril is entitled to a reward based on the value of the property rescued for putting

11. Postwar Ventures

himself and presumably his ship and crew at risk. In a court case, the "salvor" has to prove the ship and contents were in real danger and the court has to agree.

A libel suit is on the books from June 30, 1825. Burns asked the court to honor selling the rights to him for salvaging goods. He had been accused of stealing what he and a crew salvaged in goods from the cargo ship. Hart and Burns eventually came to some agreement as the cargo went to auction.

Burns continued to add to his legend on land and the local waters. He made what amounted to a citizen's arrest in a murder case in October 1825. William Johnson of New Bern was murdered, and according to the October 21, 1825, *Raleigh Register*, Burns, who was sailing from New Bern to Elizabeth City, heard of the case. Burns suspected Manuel Antonio of Portugal and "had his suspicions confirmed by one of the crew who knew Antonio." Antonio was trying to make his escape on an open boat in the sound when he was picked up by Burns and his men on their schooner. When he arrived in Elizabeth City, Burns informed the local authorities who then arrested Antonio.[27] Antonio was convicted of the murder and executed in New Bern on May 12, 1826. Claims against his will were called for in public notices in local newspapers the next month.

The *New Bern Sentinel* reported in its March 7, 1827, edition that one of Burns' enterprises in Beaufort had been denied a liquor license. In true Burns fashion, he did not let this pass lightly either—he took out a notice in the newspaper to let the public know about his runaround with local officials. The wording is priceless, calling out the local board and then inviting them to a physical confrontation, somewhat of an unusual challenge for a sitting legislator:

> To the Public.
>
> I feel it to be a duty I owe to the Public to state, that at the last County Court, (December Term, 1826,) I applied to said Court for a Retailing License; and in consequences of there not being a majority Of Magistrates on the Bench, I did not obtain it—so said the Clerk—My application for the License having been made to him. At the present Court, (March Term,

Captain Otway Burns

1827,) the Clerk stated these facts to the Honorable Grand Jury; but some of the gentlemen composing the body, Under the influence of envious and prejudiced feelings, said I ought to be indicted; whilst other gentlemen in the same town, also retailers of spirituous liquors, and who had not applied for licenses, were to be exempt from prosecution.

If this statement shall offend any of the prejudiced gentlemen to whom I allude, they are at liberty to call on me for further explanation.

OTWAY BURNS
Beaufort, Carteret County, March 7, 1827

Despite that brewing drama, however, his next big fight was over bricks. There was a river of clay that ran through Carteret County, and Burns was quick to jump on this money-making opportunity. He funded several brick kilns and encouraged locals to become skilled in masonry. Carteret County local historian Dee Lewis believes his main operation was in the community of Straits.[28] He had an interest in several brick kilns that were contracted to produce material for the army's construction of Fort Macon. The story has many turns, complicated by conflicting news stories from the day.

Beaufort had been defended by eight smoothbore cannons posted at Fort Hampton, an installation that saw service from 1808 to 1809 and then was sporadically manned until being abandoned in 1820 after damage from hurricanes and erosion. Spanish privateers caused trouble in Beaufort in the 1740s and, in August 1747, attacked and plundered the town until the citizens finally organized to drive them away. Nearby Fort Dobbs had been started in 1756 but never finished. The federal government decided to build a new structure, originally called the fort on Bogue Point; it would later be renamed Fort Macon for prominent North Carolina post–Revolutionary War statesman Nathaniel Macon. (Macon's name would also be honored with counties in North Carolina and five other states, a handful of towns, and Randolph-Macon College. Macon, who was a U.S. senator by then, was instrumental in securing funding and pushing the fort project's start. Ironically, Macon was not an advocate for change or progress, being a skeptic of steam and science, and was not a fan of moral reform or internal improvements because of the implications

11. Postwar Ventures

it might have on slavery. His politics in that regard did not align with those of Burns.) In December 1825, Lieutenant William A. Eliason, from the U.S. Army Corps of Engineers, arrived in Beaufort to oversee construction. He'd spent three years as assistant engineer at Fort Monroe in Virginia. The new fort would be built near Dobbs and Hampton on the Bogue Banks side of Beaufort Inlet.[29]

There was conflict right off the bat, with a small group of landowners refusing to sell their property to the government. Two of them had inflated the price beyond fair market value and the War Department asked Governor H.C. Burton to condemn the land using imminent domain. The legislature seized the 405 acres, and a jury of 18 men set the value at $1,287, which the federal government paid and the landowners retained fishing rights.[30] Eliason issued notices to buy brick and stone and advised the local slave owners of the opportunity to employ their slaves at 40 cents per day.[31]

Construction began in March 1826 but was halted by sea encroachments. A wharf was built on the Bogue Sound and a canal was dug from the sound to the worksite. The dirt dug from the canal was used to form the sloping edges of the fort, which was shaped like a pentagon. The foundation was finally laid by May 1827. There were not enough skilled masonry workers, which slowed things down, and additional ones were brought in from the North. The lieutenant also didn't believe the brick quality was good enough. Eliason was mainly using bricks supplied by Dr. James Manney, a doctor who had moved from New York to New Bern in 1809 and later to Beaufort, who was on the board of the Clubfoot and Harlowe Canal Company and served alongside Burns in the legislature. Another large share of the masonry came from Burns. Manney and Burns agree to adapt manufacturing processes of Northern brickyards to match Eliason's specifications, and things seemed to be going fine. At Eliason's suggestion, Burns hired a foreman from Alexandria, Virginia, and Manney also brought in more experienced workers. Eliason helped oversee the setup and start of production.[32]

In July 1827, Captain John L. Smith replaced Eliason, who remained onsite as second in command. Eliason was so well liked by the locals that they gave him a public dinner. In his remarks, Burns said, "Our distinguished guest, Lieutenant Eliason … wherever fortune may bear him, he will carry with him the affections and esteem of the citizens of Carteret."[33] Dr. Manney thanked the Corps of Engineers, and Eliason returned his thanks. Things would take a turn after Eliason's removal as the engineer in charge. The story also gets complicated as firsthand accounts of what transpired next offer a muddy view of an escalating conflict.

For their part, Eliason and Smith butted heads right away. By October, Smith had made changes in the inspection process and the types of bricks being used, excluding two previously approved types that had been ordered and accepted. The brick masons were angry, particularly Manney, who had stockpiled a large inventory ready to be delivered to the fort. The dispute between the two men went public and went from heated words to threats. Manney tried to get the other local contractors to go in with him against Smith. Smith retaliated by firing Manney as surgeon to the labor force. Manney published a derogatory article about the health conditions at Fort Macon in the *New Bern Sentinel*, which nearly led to a duel between him and Smith. Finally, Manney appealed to Congress for restitution of his losses from making Fort Macon bricks.[34] Meanwhile, Eliason and Smith's relationship deteriorated to the point that in November, Smith notified the Engineer Department that he was going to arrest Eliason and bring charges against him. He claimed the lieutenant had sided with the brickmakers against him and opposed his construction changes, which had damaged Smith's reputation. The charges were later deemed false and withdrawn.[35]

Smith apparently had problems with the subcontractors and fired many of them, eventually becoming dissatisfied with Burns as well. He didn't approve of the bricks Burns and Manney were sending. The men had delivered 600,000 bricks to the construction site, and Smith was refusing them—some were less than one-eighth of an inch off spec. Burns and Manney wrote to Army Chief Engineer

11. Postwar Ventures

Charles Gretiot and complained, while Smith threatened to stop all purchases of local bricks and instead buy from Virginia makers. The suppliers threatened to stop deliveries altogether. Manney and Burns may have been competitors, but they'd also been colleagues on boards and in the legislature and united to get rid of Smith. Smith was removed from the post and Eliason put back in charge. Burns and Manney expected a return to the previous agreement, but any notion of Eliason siding with them evaporated quickly. Gone was the goodwill of the party in Eliason's honor earlier. The lieutenant insisted on maintaining the new standards, and he'd accumulated enough bricks onsite that he felt he had the upper hand and cut the price from $8 to $7 per thousand, knowing that Burns and Manney had inventory sitting in their brickyards. Eliason signed a letter that was published in the *Newbern Spectator* on October 24 and is titled "Engineer Orders," dated October 7, 1829. Eliason reiterated that brick quality was down and he believed it was in the manufacturing process. He'd mentioned to Burns that he'd broken some of Manney's bricks over his knee. The letter is as follows:

"Engineer Orders, Fort Macon

The various orders in relation to the INSPECTION OF BRICKS at this Post, are by this Order condensed into One, viz:—

No Bricks to be merchantable but those having the Proportions below enumerated:

1st. To be 8⅛ inch long, 3⅞ wide, and 2⅜ deep, the least dimensions when burned.

2d. To be strong enough to present a fair average third capable of bearing 750 lbs. on the middle of a six inch span, (as practised).

3d. None to be received that will not bear 300 lbs. as in the 2d paragraph, so that the average under 3d and 2d paragraph, be at least 500 lbs.

4th. Bricks receivable by the paragraphs 1,2, and 3, must have 20 per cent, of good stretchers. See samples.

5th. Bricks that are fire cracked to be received at discretion.

6th. Bricks that have been wet with salt water will not be considered marketable.

WM. A. ELIASON, *Lt. of Engineers*

The Engineer Department heard from Burns and Manney and had the price restored to the previous amount, although the drama wasn't concluded.

Captain Otway Burns

TO ALL CONCERNED.

The Market at this Post will continue open at Eight Dollars per thousand for such Bricks as are conformable to the above Order.

It will be observed, that the requisitions made are the least—reasonable deviations exceeding the requisitions will be allowed.

Contracts will be entered into, when terms are made satisfactory, for from 25 to 100,000 Bricks monthly, with any individual offering.

WM. A. ELIASON, *Lt. of Engineers*"[36]

Manney and Burns became so frustrated that a war of words erupted in the local papers.

Burns and Manney cosigned a letter, "To the Public," in the October 31, 1829, edition of the *Newbern Spectator*. They wanted to give their side of the story as brick manufacturers at Beaufort and on behalf of other suppliers in Carteret County.

Their letter stated that the public would infer that orders had been made long ago to the brickmakers, but that was untrue. "No order relative to the size of bricks was communicated to us until the 8th October"—the day *after* the notice ran in the paper. Burns and Manney said they had about 400,000 bricks on hand "moulded and burned" and about 300,000 were on hand at other brickyards in the area, "which are all ruinously affected by this order." They said the Engineer Orders should have been issued March 8 before the bricks were molded. The two businessmen knew that the bricks already made would fail. The topper for them was that Eliason offered to buy the "failed" bricks at a steep discount. The other brickmakers, which now numbered nearly a dozen, agreed so they could at least recoup some of their money, but Burns and Manney, the two biggest suppliers, dug in.

The letter stated that in June, the engineer told Burns his bricks were "rather small," and Burns immediately had new molds made to the dimensions given to him. Burns delivered 400,000 bricks and was not told they were too small until October 10. Manney's molds were altered onsite at Fort Macon under the engineer's direction and ironed at his blacksmith's shop. Eventually, orders were issued to accept the bricks from Burns and Manney. In a letter to Gretiot,

11. Postwar Ventures

An 1863 sketch of Fort Macon from Herbert Eugene Valentine's *Sketches of Civil War Scenes* **(National Archives).**

Burns wrote, "The inspection is now so sized that the business is ruinous and all concern'd in making bricks will be compell'd to quit the business." Burns also wrote in a letter that "Lt. Eliason is a difficult man to deal with, and has had disputes and difficulties with almost everyone who has had any dealings with him."[37] This was quite a turnaround from the public remarks given about Eliason two years earlier.

Manney delivered half a million bricks that summer and another 100,000 in September with no objections to their size. Burns ended up providing over 2 million bricks for the project.[38]

Apparently, the engineer had invented a new machine for trying the strength of bricks that was not being used at any other works in the country. It would require a week to measure and inspect all the bricks under new regulations. The two men wrote that they had been told in the spring that no alterations would be made in the inspection process for the current season and that all specifications would be the same as the previous year. "It is hardly necessary to say that we have been woefully disappointed in this expectation." They went on to lay out the economics of the situation as well, saying that they could deliver three-quarters of a kiln previously and were now limited to one-third. Where they were getting $8 per thousand, it now amounted to $2.66 ⅔ per thousand. "We have been extremely reluctant to have any difference with the Engineer—but his present orders are so cruel and unjust—so ruinous to our interests, that we have determined to resist them to the last extremity." The Engineering Department was considering a transfer of Eliason to defuse the situation and get the fort built. At about the same time, one of Eliason's children died, and the army removed him his posting. However, they decided to restore the previous antagonist, Smith, to the role, but apparently his approach changed while he was away, as there was no further conflict with the bricks upon his return.

In 1830, a violent gale clogged the canal and damaged the beach, again causing delays in the construction. Finally, most of the brickwork was done by December 1832. Smith turned the fort over to Lieutenant George Dutton in 1833. It took another year to make the casemates livable. The final cost was over $350,000 (other reports put the costs at over $450,000). The only problem was that the army neglected to arm the fort, and the company that finally arrived to man it ended up being transferred to Florida. It was ungarrisoned from 1836 to 1842, manned only by a sole ordnance sergeant.[39]

Despite the kerfuffle, the bricks must have been well made, as the fort served through several wars and is a historic site and tourist attraction to this day nearly 200 years later.

Burns continued to build ships during this time, rolling off the brig *Henry* from his shipyard in 1831, built from Shackleford Banks and Bogue Banks live oak. The ship plied the waters to the West Indies and as far as South Africa. He also built a small, two-masted sailboat he named the *Snap Dragon*. It was one of the first to have a

11. Postwar Ventures

centerboard in the area, was easy to maneuver, and Burns boasted it "could beat any boat in Core Sound."

Clouds were forming over Burns' far-flung enterprises, however. Several businesses in which he had invested folded, with mortgages and debts to Burns unpaid. In the mid–1830s, the federal banking system collapsed, and the old privateer doubled down by trying to help his friends cover their debts. The combination of poor management and generosity, combined with the Panic of 1837 and the ensuing depression, put the squeeze on him. At least nine mortgage deeds were executed by him in Carteret County between 1821 and 1834 as his debts piled up. Despite his mounting financial troubles, Burns continued to serve his community and, along with Manney, took part in a September 1833 exam of the bar and harbor of Beaufort. The committee, with representatives from Craven, Beaufort, and Pitt counties as well as two pilots, found that the channel was straight and "sufficiently capacious for a fleet of three hundred sail to moor in safely" and "that the harbor is well protected from tempests, and has good anchoring ground. It is protected by fortifications, the general government having just completed a work which has entire command of it."[40]

Despite his wealth, Burns had borrowed heavily in the 1830s, using his holdings as collateral. His loyalty was misplaced as no one came to his aid. Even as Yancey County was naming its county seat Burnsville in 1834, Burns was facing financial disaster. By 1840, he was broke.

12

The Legislator

BURNS RODE HIS LEGENDARY WAR record and regional popularity into politics in 1822, winning a seat to represent Carteret County in the North Carolina House of Commons, where he was joined by Isaac Hellen. He arrived in Raleigh, which had been the state capital for 30 years and was growing by leaps and bounds, ready to work to drag the state into a more modern era.

Burns ended up serving in the North Carolina House of Commons from 1821 to 1822, 1824 to 1828, and 1832 to 1833. He served in the state senate from 1828 to 1830 and 1833 to 1835. Burns was a Democrat who admired Andrew Jackson, was known for his "enlightened" views, and for supporting what he thought was right, regardless of the consequences. Burns was an advocate for public transportation and for economic development. He wanted turnpikes built and advocated to improve the navigation of the Cape Fear and Deep Rivers, which both run from central North Carolina to Wilmington (the Deep and Haw join to form the Cape Fear) and worked to help the railroads get charters. He wanted a road built from Fayetteville in the east to Wilkesboro in the west and wanted to drain Lake Mattamuskeet as well as many of the eastern swamps. He wanted to wake North Carolina from its sleepy status quo and promote growth through economic development. This meant focusing on internal improvements to transport people and cargo quicker and more efficiently.

One of the planks in his platform was to improve the state's infrastructure, including local waterways, naturally because of his experience as a merchantman. Edgar Stanton Maclay, who wrote

12. The Legislator

Painting of the North Carolina State House, 1818, by Jacob Marling (courtesy State Archives of North Carolina).

several pieces about Burns, said his "fearlessness and humanity which characterized his conduct in the war" was the same tact he followed in the political arena. He was praised by fellow legislator William H. Battle for "his independence and freedom from demagoguery" and backed by a "disposition to answer supposed insults with the strong argument of ponderous fists."[1] Burns never ruled out violence, or the threat of it, to resolve a problem. That political disposition served Burns well until it didn't.

In 1823, construction of the Clubfoot Creek to Harlowe Creek Canal finally got underway. This waterway was designed to connect the Neuse and Newport Rivers, and Burns would be involved in it both as a legislator and director. It had been planned since 1766, but it took almost 50 years to start. The canal was promoted as a way to lower shipping costs and aid farmers.[2] It took four years to build the six-mile canal, and when completed, it was a busy and successful waterway early on.

However, it seemed like there were always more than a few challenges for the waterway. From the beginning, there were troubles with not enough water and a lack of traffic that caused sawmills and brickyards to close. Toll revenues dropped steadily from $746 in 1829 to $347 in 1833, when repairs were needed.[3] Clubfoot and Harlowe Creek Canal Company was listed for sale and had financial issues in 1844, was foreclosed on, reorganized, and was back in operation by 1849. An attempt to sell it was made in 1845, but no buyers could be found. A new canal was dug next to the original in 1885.

However, Burns' biggest vote that year was for the establishment of Davidson County in the western half of the state. Voting for the right thing eventually offered harsh political consequences for Burns. There was a disparity in representation in North Carolina in the early 19th century. Eastern North Carolina controlled about two-thirds of the voting power in the legislature and intended to keep that control. When western representatives brought forth bills to create new counties, the east simply voted against them. Not only did counties have representatives, but some borough towns—almost all in the east—did as well. The legislature picked the governor, the supreme court justices, and the superior court judges. When the west called for a new county, the eastern power brokers either voted it down or created a new eastern county to keep the scales tipped in their favor.[4] The western counties raised a ruckus about the lack of representation, but those in power rarely are willing to share it. It caused rifts so serious that it threatened the state's sovereignty at one point. Governor David L. Swain, from Buncombe County, even warned that the west might determine to secede if things didn't change.

Burns didn't go along with this disparity and, as with most other things in his life, followed his gut, what he thought was right—just like when he captained the *Snap Dragon*. It would ultimately extract a high political cost. He was a man of the people at heart.

12. The Legislator

As he fell into more debt while also being a loaner of money, he sought protections for debtors. He opposed efforts to weaken the newly established North Carolina Supreme Court and tried to stop efforts to drive away banks with excessive taxes. Burns also saw potential in the Wilmington area and felt that if the river could be deepened below the growing city, the area would boom with shipping. Burns supported agriculture and manufacturing bills. Such "enlightened," radical views did not sit well with opposing parties and even some in his own party.

In 1824, Burns was reelected to the House with W.D. Styron. He was appointed to the Committee for Internal Improvements. Burns wanted to advance what the *North Carolina Farmer* would later call the "Rip Van Winkle State" and actually faced opposition from many lawmakers who wanted to keep the state as it was—an undeveloped backwater. While Burns was in the House, "a legislative committee reported that North Carolina was 'a state without foreign commerce,' for want of seaports or a staple; without internal communication by rivers, roads, or canals; without a cash market for any article of agricultural product; without manufactures; in short, without any object to which native industry and active enterprise could be directed."[5] There was an effort by some lawmakers to repeal an 1819 act to fund internal improvements, but that was defeated by Burns and others like him. Some of the accomplishments were roads in places from Tyrell County at the coast to the Smoky Mountain Turnpike and work on the 22-mile Great Dismal Swamp canal, which had been completed in 1805. The legislature was a busy place in those days. In addition to electing the governor, senators, judges, and other local officials were tapped, and they voted on matters as small as individual petitions for divorces for the entire state. They also faced larger issues that would haunt the state for decades to come. In November, the Manumission Society made a presentation for the gradual abolition of slavery. The body referred the proposal to a "special committee."

Captain Otway Burns

Burns continued to represent Carteret County in the House in 1825, along with William H. Borden. Burns presented a bill for that session to amend an 1813 law about how persons injured by erection of public mills could attempt to recover damages. He also supported a bill to establish a medical society to regulate surgery, which was also met with significant opposition.

Burns was reelected to the House with Elijah Bell in 1826. He put up a bill to increase the capital stock of the Clubfoot and Harlowe Creek Canal Company to provide aid to finish the canal. He put forth a bill that sounds odd today—one that called for someone to be appointed to "take charge of the State House during the recess of the Legislature" to keep the doors locked unless there were visitors or there was "airing of the apartments" to preserve the furniture and fixtures and provide coverings for the chandeliers and curtains. Another major internal improvement to stir in the House of Commons was a bill to improve the navigation of the Cape Fear River below Wilmington.

Burns also had one of his several controversial stances that year. A bill was presented to prevent free persons of color from migrating to North Carolina, and he was one of several representatives to vote against the bill, which passed.

Burns returned to the House of Commons with David Borden in the 1827–1828 session. A committee was formed jointly with the Senate to examine and settle the accounts of the Clubfoot and Harlowe Creek Canal Company, and Burns was appointed to serve. He was also added to the Divorce and Alimony Committee; later in the session, jurisdiction for divorces was handed over to superior courts. A bill was passed requiring clergy and other officiants to send marriage licenses to the county clerks. There was a movement to allow freemen to elect county sheriffs, which was postponed for a vote after a tie in the House resulted in the Speaker voting against it. In the same session, Burns proposed a bill to amend the wreck laws regarding shipping in the state's coastal waters as it applied to Carteret County.

12. The Legislator

The Internal Improvements Committee recommended a turnpike be built in Burke County, and $6,252 was approved to improve navigation of Cape Fear River. Burns was appointed as one of the superintendents for balloting for the election of four University of North Carolina trustees. There was a resolution from the House to instruct the governor to inform the secretary of war of the desire for a railroad line from New Bern to Raleigh to be built by the U.S. Army Corps of Engineers. There was also a move from the Internal Improvements Committee to survey for a railroad from Yadkin County to Fayetteville; both the resolution and the bill were postponed, and a resolution from Burns to authorize the committee to make examinations and surveys as "deemed expedient and proper" was also rejected. Also of note that session was monies approved to cover the expenses for a reception honoring visiting darling of the revolution General Lafayette.

The biggest vote that year was for the establishment of Macon County out of parts of Burke and Buncombe in western North Carolina. Burns was a key vote in getting Macon County approved—the final vote was 63–61. Also in the 1827–28 session, he cast the tying vote at 62–62 for the approval of Yancey County, and the Speaker of the House voted yes to send the bill to the Senate, where it was defeated.

Burns went to the Senate in 1828, narrowly defeating Adams candidate Benjamin Leecraft 203–194. Burns supported a bill that any slave over 50 who was emancipated did not have to leave the state if he or she had performed "meritorious services." Another $6,000 was approved for the Clubfoot and Harlowe Creek Canal. A bill moved to build a road in the coastal county of Tyrell, and Burns proposed a bill for funding the Internal Improvements Committee and hiring a state engineer. He was also put on a committee as a superintendent of the balloting for governor. In an odd move, Burns voted for postponement of consideration for a bill that would make for stronger punishments for people who poisoned others. His effort failed, and the bill passed. His most important vote of the session was again for more representation of western North Carolinians. He had an important vote in getting Cherokee County approved, 63–61. Burns was also an admirer and campaigner for Andrew Jackson, and in 1828 when Jackson made his first bid for the presidency, Burns was named as a delegate "to attend any meeting which may be held at Raleigh, or elsewhere, for the purpose of forming a Jackson Electoral Ticket."[6] This powerful ally would prove to be vital later in his life.

Burns was reelected in 1829. The Internal Improvements Committee recommended opening and improving Currituck Inlet, and Burns was placed on a committee to consider connecting the Neuse River with Beaufort harbor. The bill to create Yancey County came up again but failed to make it through both chambers. The legislature did pass a bill to classify Quakers, Moravians, Dunkards, and Menonists on "equal footing with other free men." It wasn't just new counties that Burns supported. He was an early proponent of railroads and canals, but since the easternmost counties had many rivers to move goods, those in power typically voted against railroads. As a senator, he was appointed to the Board of Internal Improvements in January 1829, along with Cadwallader Jones, James Mebane, Andrew Joiner, James McKay, and Marsden Campbell. Bills seeing movement were to repair the State House and railing the public square; amending an act from 1819 appointing commissioners in Chapel Hill; addressing the Wardens of the Poor of Lincoln and "more effectual administration of justice in the county courts of Duplin; incorporation of the Swannanoa and Laurel River Turnpike Company; and 'the bank question.'" A bill compelling sheriffs to advertise elections in the state was rejected.[7]

Many sources list Burns as continuously serving in the legislature, but official Senate and House records list David W. Borden as the senator from Carteret and Thomas Marshall and John F. Jones as representatives in the House. In the 1831 records, Carteret's listing for Senate is blank. Burns, despite taking ill, was made chair of the Committee for Internal Improvements from the area. At a meeting on November 26, 1831, at the Carteret County Courthouse in

12. The Legislator

Beaufort, there was a discussion among the members that lack of infrastructure in the state was causing a mass emigration of citizens. A resolution was passed saying that without improvements, North Carolina "will be behind every state in the Union in wealth and population ... and that a system of Internal Improvements is the only means of staying the tide of emigration which is almost depopulating the state." A call was made to coordinate with a Salisbury-based committee hoping to push for improvements as well.[8] The state capitol building burned that year.

In 1832, Burns is listed as being in the House of Commons with Borden. He submitted a resolution that called for North Carolina to prepare for war because he felt the state could be involved and forced to rely on its own defense before getting aid from the "general government." This had certainly been the case 20 years earlier when the British landed on the Outer Banks. The North Carolina coast was still largely unprotected. This sentiment would prove prophetic decades later when the Civil War started and the state's coastline would be practically defenseless. Burns called for the state to gather and mount artillery, procure ammunition, buy equipment, and augment the state's troops. Lawmakers voted to rebuild the burned-out capitol that year—it would take nine years to finish the project, a building still in use today (although not for the legislature). A bill to build the Cape Fear and Yadkin Railroad Company passed the House with Burns' support, as did a bill to prevent the unlawful transportation of slaves from the state.

In the 1833–34 session, Burns was back in the Senate with Elijah Bell and Dr. James Manney filling the county's House seats. That term, he was appointed to a committee to "look into" the state banks, the Bank of New Bern and the Bank of Cape Fear, to see the dividends, paper notes, and debts due "that may throw light upon this matter." Some internal infrastructure that Burns and other legislators sought and campaigned on to help improve the North Carolina economy started to take place at last. Finally, in 1833, Yancey County was established by a 33–28 vote. The citizenry was so thankful that they named their county seat after the privateer, and today there is a statue in Burnsville that celebrates the man. The *New Bern Sentinel* reported, "It appears from the *Rutherford Spectator* that the metropolis of the new county of Yancey is to be christened Burnsville 'after Otway Burns, the Senator from Carteret,—the hero of the *Snap Dragon* during the last war, and the undeviating friend of all the just measures of the West.'" The paper went on to say, "Long life and prosperity to this infant star thus added to the twinkling galaxy which bespangles the gown of our good old mother. May the sons of Burnsville, like their intrepid favourite be always ready to Stand for their country's glory fast, And nail her colours to the mast."[9] A reform movement started in 1833, and a bill for a convention made its way through the legislature and was argued in 1834 for "an act concerning a convention to amend the constitution of the state." The Convention of 1835 was called, and the *Semi-Weekly Standard* in Raleigh reported years later that there was a "compromise which was made by a few patriotic eastern legislators with their western brethren."[10] One of the big issues at stake was giving more representation to the western part of the state, something many of the wealthy powerbrokers in the east opposed. There were rumblings that if they could not achieve more equitable representation, the western counties might seek to form another state. However, a group of easterners were willing to push back on this. In the Senate, Burns from Carteret, Spaight of Craven, William B. Lockhardt of Wilmington, James Wyche of Granville, and A. Mebane of Bertie were for the change. In the House, William H. Hawood, Jr., of Wake; Elijah Bell and James Manney of Carteret; Sandy Harris of Granville; Abner Hartley and Fred P. Latham of Craven; George Whitfield of Lenoir; Edward B. Dudley of Wilmington; Fred Norcom of Edenton; Matthew Manley of New Bern; and Thomas Ownsby of Halifax were on board. These eastern members agreed that if the western legislators would accept taxation as the basis of representation in the Senate and federal numbers as the basis of representation in the House, "they would put it in the power of the majority of the people living in the west to call

12. The Legislator

a convention under the sanction of law ... a mode of amending the constitution." There was a caveat that the eastern lawmakers insisted on: that any changes to the state constitution protected slave property "which they considered so essential to their safety."[11] The Senate passed the bill 31–30, with Burns casting the deciding vote, and it squeaked by 66–64 in the House. Eastern politicians publicly referred to him as a "traitor."

That same year, the legislature passed an act to establish the Bank of North Carolina and opened subscriptions for stock of $1 million in $100 shares. Commissioners were appointed at various locations across the state. Burns, Thomas Marshall, David W. Borden, Jeconias Piggott, and Benjamin Leecraft were appointed to serve at Beaufort by Swain, and commissioners were added at Wilmington, Fayetteville, New Bern, Washington, Halifax, Elizabeth City, Tarboro, Raleigh, Hillsborough, Milton, Greensboro, Salem, Salisbury, Wadesboro, Charlotte, Lincolnton, Wilkesboro, Morganton, and Asheville.[12]

In February 1834, Burns was appointed a commissioner in the Clubfoot and Harlowe Creek Canal Company with five shares of stock. Other commissioners were Dr. James Manney, Joseph Borden, Jechonias Pigott, and Elijah Pigott. The directors were Alexander Henderson and M.C. Stephens.[13] In 1834, his Senate seat was contested back in Carteret County. The Senate took up a resolution declaring that Burns was entitled to keep his seat in the chamber. George W. Montgomery of Hertford tried to amend the resolution by inserting the word "not" after the word "is." His hijinks were foiled by a 42–16 vote. After a couple of other resolutions failed, a resolution to end any more challenges of the election and award the seat to Burns was passed by a 44–14 vote.[14] In what would be his final term, Burns voted for a bill to repeal the literacy restriction and ban on preaching for slaves. That same year, a report was submitted to the legislature on the harbor at Beaufort concerning what improvements needed to be made, and a bill was proposed in the House for a

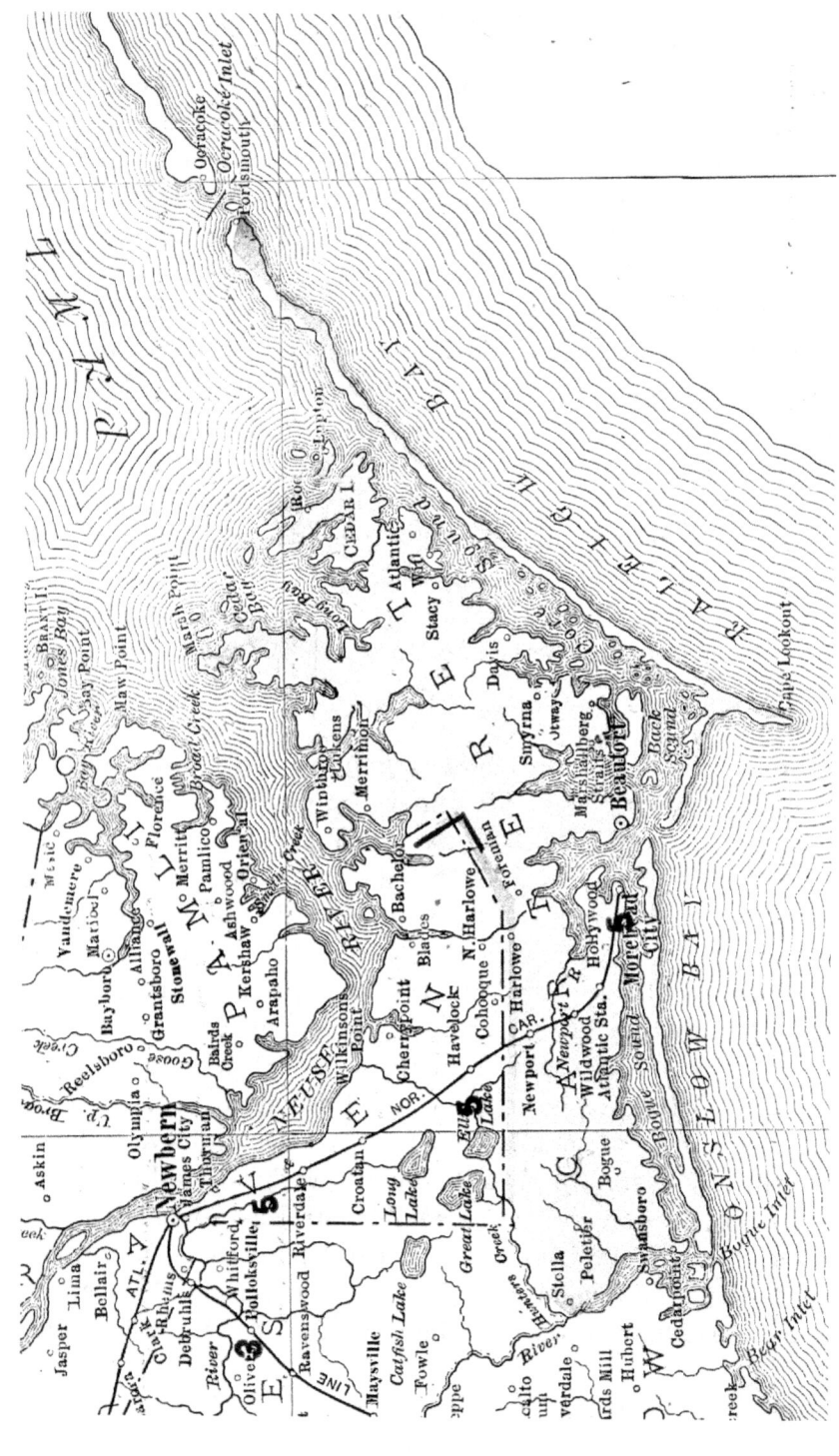

12. The Legislator

railroad that would run from Beaufort to Tennessee; it did not make it into law.[15]

Burns still had slaves, but as early as 1824, he went on record as favoring some method to free them, likely because of his experience with Black sailors. He supported proposals that protected freed slaves and legislation to allow slave owners to emancipate their slaves—even though he had not emancipated his own. He voted against laws that prohibited free Blacks from other states from settling in North Carolina. He wanted to repeal laws that prohibited Blacks from getting an education and being able to freely practice religion.[16] He also wanted election of local sheriffs and clerk courts instead of appointments and wanted to break up the old "courthouse rings" of governing. He was defeated by James W. Bryan in his last election. He was active as a lawmaker to the very end. A few years after Burns' lawmaking career ended, the Raleigh & Gaston Railroad was completed, and between 1840 and 1850, the population of the city doubled. Improved infrastructure did produce growth, as he believed. As his political fortunes spiraled downward, so did his personal life.

Years later, Captain S.A. Ashe wrote about Burns' tenure as a legislator and how difficult it was to take a stand for western representation in the legislature in the August 16, 1903, *Raleigh News and Observer*: "Readers would hardly believe how intense and bitter was the feeling between the sections ... by his vote he destroyed himself and never afterwards lifted up his head politically."[17] Indeed, Burns' political career was over and he returned home. It would not be a quiet withdrawal from public life that followed, nor would it be without adventure and personal mayhem.

Opposite: This 1905 Rand McNally map shows Otway Burns' main area of operations in Swansboro, New Bern, Beaufort, and Portsmouth Island. The area of the Clubfoot and Harlow Creek Canal can be seen as well as the community that bears the captain's first name (Library of Congress).

13

Hard Times

For Burns, the money problems started during his political career and caused him to have to sell most of his property. On January 21, 1831, he sold eight properties and nine slaves to pay debts. He had more than one court appearance in Carteret County to answer for debts totaling $6,000 to 15 people.[1] He continued to liquidate assets over the next few years until his entire fortune was gone. He had at least nine mortgages on the books in the county from 1821 to 1834.[2] The hard economic times of the late 1830s, including the Panic of 1837, finished Burns off.

There wasn't much relief to be had until finally his political connections came through for him. In 1835, President Andrew Jackson appointed him as keeper of the Brant Island lightship near Portsmouth Island. This kept Burns from being homeless, and it was a job he held for 15 years until he died. It paid $500 a year.

Lightships came about in the early 1800s to supplement lighthouses and were mostly used where lighthouse construction would be impossible or at least impractical. They were ungraceful but sturdy and placed in areas that couldn't be marked with a fixed structure. The ships were anchored in place and the crews remained aboard in all weather conditions. The program was overseen by the U.S. Treasury Department until 1852, when the Lighthouse Board assumed control. It was succeeded by the U.S. Lighthouse Service in 1910 and, finally, the U.S. Coast Guard in 1939.

The ships were numbered sequentially according to construction and identified by color codes, lights, foghorn or radio signals, and large letters on the sides.[3] There were 14 in North Carolina

13. Hard Times

waters. The Brant Island lightship was in service from 1831 to 1853, before it was eventually replaced by a lighthouse. Its location was the "southern section of the Pamlico Sound, off the point of Brant Island Shoal 15 miles bearing 276 degrees from Ocracoke Light." The exposed location was in the middle of Pamlico Sound and it was constantly battered by gales. Burns requested a larger ship several times, but it was never appropriated by Congress.

Burns' second wife, Jane Hall Burns, died on October 24, 1839, and was buried in Beaufort at the Old Burying Ground. In July 1840, Burns bought a two-story house with a kitchen and outbuildings from John Rumley for $1,000. Otway mortgaged his home on Portsmouth that same year for $700 to his son, Owen. Owen took possession of the house in July 1840 and later mortgaged it himself in February 1849.[4] On February 22, 1842, Otway married for the third and final time, taking Jane Smith of Smyrna as his bride. She moved out to Portsmouth Island with Burns. The old captain outlived her as well.

In 1843, years after Burns left politics, there was a nasty congressional election, but it showed the old captain still had some popularity and political influence. Archibald H. Arrington of Nash County was elected to Congress with help from Burns. The election also showed that Burns still had enemies as well. The next year, Whigs charged him with neglecting his duties and withholding wages from his crew members and attempted to have him removed as lightkeeper of Brant Island. An article in the *Fayetteville Weekly Observer* of July 16, 1845, complained that three lightkeepers had been removed from posts because they were Whigs and not because of their performance. The article disparaged their successors and then took aim at Burns, accusing him of being an alcoholic and derelict of duty: "Now look on this picture: Otway Burns (the man who carries about that red nose) has not been on board the Boat which he is Keeper for nearly five months. Yet he is kept in office and receives his pay, because he is a Locofoen, while worthy men who attend faithfully to their duties are turned out, because they are Whigs!

Captain Otway Burns

This is justice—Democratic justice."[5] Locofocos were a faction of the Democratic Party in the 1830s and '40s in opposition to the "Tammany Hall" gang in New York. They were fans of Andrew Jackson, free trade, and protections for labor unions and were against paper money and state banks. They originally called themselves the Equal Rights Party. The nickname came from a brand of self-igniting cigar called loco-foco, which became a generic term for "self-igniting" matches.

The old captain was outraged, as mad as he'd been about charges of piracy nearly 40 years before. He still had plenty of fight, especially when his good name—battered as it was—was at stake. He traveled to Washington, D.C., to argue his case in person to Treasury Department officials.[6] He was cleared after an investigation revealed the charges were without merit and politically motivated.[7]

Portsmouth Island is today a deserted island with no residents, a ghost town with a few buildings still standing, visited irregularly by curious history tourists and photographers. However, when Burns—broke—was living with the family of John L. Hunter, it was a port of entry and a hopping town of about 1,000 souls. It was established in 1753 by the North Carolina General Assembly and, by 1770, was the largest settlement on the Outer Banks. It was a major shipping center for nearly a century. Ocracoke Inlet was the major trade route from the Outer Banks to North Carolina's ports, and large, heavy ships were too big for the inlet and had to transfer their cargo to lighter, shallow draft boats called "lightering ships." In 1842, two-thirds of all North Carolina exports passed through Portsmouth.[8]

Mother nature and the turbulent times combined to change the importance of the place. Many citizens fled during the Civil War, and the area started shoaling. A storm later opened a bigger and deeper inlet at Hatteras in 1846, which caused traffic to begin shifting. It was still a fishing village in 1894 when the U.S. Lifesaving Service took over, but by 1956, the population was down to 17. The lifesaving service was decommissioned in 1937. Finally, in 1971, the last two

13. Hard Times

residents moved inland. Today, the island is part of the Cape Lookout National Seashore under the care of the National Park Service.

Jane Smith Burns died at some point before Otway, but it is not clear when, as she is not listed on the 1850 census, which listed only Otway living as a mariner "in his dotage."[9] On October 25, 1850, Burns died at the Hunter home on Portsmouth, where he was living. There was a report that some men from Portsmouth took Burns' body to Beaufort and dumped it "unboxed upon the wharf." An onlooker said dryly, "But if this be true it does not bother Otway one bit."[10] Local historian Dee Lewis said that one local legend was that the men told those on the docks, "Here's your hero," as they dumped the remains on the dock. He was buried in the Old Burying Ground in Beaufort on Ann Street next to his second wife without a ceremony and initially without a grave marker being erected.

Later, a cannon purported to be from the *Snap Dragon* was placed atop his headstone and remains to this day. But even that story suffers from conflicting reports. The *Charlotte News* reported in its February 7, 1901, edition that "a big rusty cannon lying on Broad Street in front of J.K. Willis' marble works ... is a cannon from the privateer Snapdragon." The story went on to say that the cannon had been used as a landmark in Beaufort and that Otway's grandson Walter Francis Burns obtained the cannon from the town to be placed on Otway's grave, which was unmarked at the time. It noted that the cannon was to be mounted on top of a block of Georgia marble as a "handsome and appropriate mark of the resting place of the bold privateersman."[11]

However, a report in the *Daily Journal* of New Bern on February 8, 1901, disputes that. The story mentions "two cannon at the northeast corner of Pollock and Middle streets" and claims they are not from the *Snap Dragon* as widely believed but go back to the Revolutionary War from a ship owned by John Wright Stanley captured by the British. The story said that the name "Lady Blessington" had been engraved on the breech of one of the guns but had been worn away. It further said that when Walter Burns visited the

Captain Otway Burns

area in 1900, he wanted to have those guns and one from Jacksonville mounted on the courthouse grounds and that he offered to "bear half the expense," up to $5,000, for a "handsome monument" honoring Otway if the town and/or county would pay the rest and that Walter "appears to have thought that the guns were connected with the history of his grandfather."[12] If the guns were from the *Snap Dragon*, they would have had to have been removed before the fourth and final voyage of the ship as it was captured and later auctioned, never to return to North Carolina, before eventually being lost at sea.

On Monday, July 5, 1901, a dedication ceremony for the Burns grave marker in Beaufort was held with the cannon that Walter had worked so hard to get in place. Newspaper reports said a crowd of more than 5,000 people turned out, including 250 Masons who held a ceremony that "consecrated the monument to Burns as a patron of the order." The marker's inscription was simple: "CAPT. OTWAY BURNS. / Son of Francis Burns. / Commander United States Privateer. / SNAP DRAGON / War 1812–15. / Born in Onslow County N.C. / 1775. / Died at Portsmouth N.C. / 1850. / BURNS."[13]

14

Legacy of Legends and Lies

THE MUSEUM AT THE SWANSBORO Area Heritage Center not far from where Otway grew up has a display that describes Burns as a man who "embodied the spirit of adventure and patriotism" and adds that he was a famous man in his time and was still being mentioned regularly in newspapers from the 1870s to the 1890s. Groups of schoolchildren used to make visits to his Beaufort grave before Burns fell out of public history's view. Few outside of down east coastal North Carolina have heard of him.

A man who lives an adventurous and outsized life will almost always leave behind a legacy of legends and lies. Otway Burns is no exception. Most stories run from the outlandish to the ridiculous but were repeated publicly so many times that they've managed to stick around for over 100 years in some cases, and many have become accepted as truth.

Perhaps the most scandalous of the tall tales involving the captain were related to Theodosia Burr Alston. Alston was the daughter of former Vice President Aaron Burr and the wife of the newly elected governor of South Carolina in 1812, John Alston, whom she had married in 1801. Theodosia was planning to travel to New York to see her father, who was returning from exile after the deadly duel that resulted in the death of Alexander Hamilton and later the plot to create his own country on the western frontier. Theodosia and her husband had actually assisted Burr in his escape and helped smuggle him out of the country after his plot to provoke a rebellion in the Southwest United States and establish himself as the leader was exposed by a co-conspirator.

Captain Otway Burns

She booked passage on the *Patriot*, a former—and possibly still-active—privateer out of Georgetown, South Carolina, and departed on December 31, 1812. The former privateer captain of the ship was William Overstocks. For this voyage, the name was painted over, all guns were taken below decks, and a different captain was put in charge. Some believe the cargo on board was plunder from Overstocks' privateering days that he wanted to get to New York quickly and sell.

The ship disappeared at sea, and neither it nor anyone aboard was ever seen or heard from again. Sailors, locals, and others did not let the mystery lie. Several theories and legends emerged over the years including the following:

- "Bankers," sometimes called "wreckers," were local men who salvaged shipwrecks on the North Carolina Outer Banks—also known as the Graveyard of the Atlantic—and were often accused of nefarious deeds. It is said that when "business" was slow, these men would lead a horse with a lantern tied around its neck along the beaches to confuse captains and cause ships to wreck. This is one of the legends of how Nags Head got its name.

It's said that after luring the *Patriot* to wreck and taking the cargo, these men killed the crew and passengers and that Theodosia may have fallen victim along with others. This story seems unlikely and has largely been discredited.

- One story reported that pirates captured the ship and murdered everyone on board.
- Another legend says that Theodosia survived the shipwreck and was found by a local Indian. She was said to be naked, wearing only a locket. He rescued her and then she died in his arms after saying her father had been a white man chief who had left the land because people misunderstood him. The Indian wore the locket inscribed with the name "Theodosia" from that point on.

14. Legacy of Legends and Lies

- *Fernando de Lemos, Truth and Fiction*, a novel published in 1872 by Charles Gayarré, devoted a chapter to a ship captured by pirates off Cape Hatteras who made a beautiful woman walk the plank. Gayarré was a former secretary of state of Louisiana.
- One story claims that Theodosia survived the shipwreck and was the mysterious woman who died in Gadsby's Tavern in Alexandria, Virginia, on October 14, 1816, and is a mystery/ghost story in its own right. However, the "Female Stranger" was much older than Theodosia Burr would have been.
- Carteret County historian Dee Lewis said there is also a legend that Theodosia survived whatever happened to her and married a criminal on the Outer Banks and lived out her days there.

While there are countless other tales, perhaps the craziest one accuses Burns of being responsible. The story goes that while working as a privateer, Burns took the former *Patriot*, killed all on board, and made off with the cargo. He supposedly made Theodosia walk the plank. While Burns considered himself a patriot and would most likely not have liked Aaron Burr, this story has holes all through it and is a complete fabrication pushed through a couple of letters published in newspapers long after the passing of Burns.

First, according to ship records, Burns would have been off the coast of South America during the time Theodosia's ship would have been off the North Carolina coast. This is not to mention the fact that Burns did not operate in this way during any part of the war or any other time for that matter, and it is unlikely he would have taken such action against another American privateer or a passenger. He was known for conducting his ship with honor, even by his adversaries' accounts, and there is no record of murderous or barbaric behavior toward the British or Spanish he encountered.

Connected to the story is that of the mystery portrait. A letter in the *Daily Journal* of New Bern on December 24, 1895, from Major

Captain Otway Burns

Graham Daves referenced a previous story about relics that would be good contributions to the upcoming East Carolina Fair. One of those relics was in the possession of Mrs. J.P. Overman of Elizabeth City at the time—the oil portrait believed to be of Theodosia. Overman had obtained the portrait from a Mrs. Tillitt, who lived on the beach and told of the portrait being found in the wreck of a ship attacked by pirates. It was said that through "much correspondence" with the Alston family, it was determined the woman "bore great resemblance to the deceased lady."[1] Daves argued that Burns and his crew were too well known to have committed an act of piracy on Theodosia's ship and that Burns was too prominent a figure during the war.

In his book *Graveyard of the Atlantic*, David Stick wrote that the ship was lost off the shore of North Carolina with all on board dying. Investigations were carried out all the way to Nassau, Bahamas, to find it. Several men over the years confessed to being part of the attack on the *Patriot*, but an interesting twist took place in 1869 and a story that differs slightly from the one related by Daves. Dr. William Gaskins Pool of Elizabeth City, who was on vacation near Nags Head, was attending to a patient named Polly Mann.[2] Mann had an oil portrait on the wall of her Outer Banks cottage, which was so well done it seemed out of place to the doctor. The doctor's daughter Anna, who had gone along on the house call, said she saw a portrait "of a beautiful young woman about twenty five years of age."[3] He took the portrait, which is believed to be painted by John Vanderlyn, as payment for his services, and it was said Burr relatives came to examine it and believed it was Theodosia.[4] This would put the wreck happening about two miles south of Nags Head.[5]

There are numerous other accounts of the Burr portrait, the most detailed was handed to me by locals in Morehead City. I couldn't source all the story, but some of the narrative was written by Van Potter.

Supposedly, a "wrecker" ended up with the painting after a successful day at work and gave it to his "best girl." Years later, around 1854, when she was elderly and sick, she gave it as payment to a

14. Legacy of Legends and Lies

doctor who had crossed the Albemarle Sound from Elizabeth City to take care of her. The woman told the doctor the story behind the portrait and he believed it could be Burr (Alston). Burr's descendants were contacted, and they compared the likeness to other images they had, and all concluded it was Theodosia. Sometime before 1933, Anna sold the portrait to a New York gallery and it was bought by a descendant of the Burr family. Eventually, the portrait made its way to the Long Island home of the Pratts, a wealthy oil family, and the portrait became known as the "Nags Harbor Theodosia Burr." It was later donated to the Lewis Walpole Library at Yale University.[6] In recent years, the portrait was brought to Elizabeth City and exhibited again at the Museum of the Albemarle.

Potter wrote that he visited his grandmother in 1901 in Beaufort, and after visiting Burns' grave, he noted that the "old cannon at the low water mark had been taken up and placed on the tomb by descendants of Burns." He said that about 2,000 people had attended the ceremony. He asked his grandmother what she remembered about the privateer from her childhood. "He was nothing but a pirate!" Potter recalled and said that's all she would say. Thirty years later, Potter was visiting with an uncle in Beaufort, the son of his grandmother, and asked what he knew about Burns. The uncle had been born in 1847, just a couple of years before Burns' death. The uncle claimed he was one of the many people in Beaufort keeping a secret and that Potter was the first person he was going to share with about Burr and Burns. He claimed that a few weeks after Theodosia sailed that the *Snap Dragon* arrived in port and that members of the crew came ashore "drunk as lords, and many of them parading the streets in women's finery!"—purporting that the clothes belonged to Theodosia. Burns' men as cross-dressing pirates has no other reference anywhere I could find; this seems more like what we'd call an internet troll today. The uncle also related that members of the community were always terrified of the *Snap Dragon* and lived in fear that Burns and his men would bombard the town. This story defies all reason and lacks any historical evidence.

Captain Otway Burns

There is a letter in the South Caroliniana Library at the University of South Carolina in Columbia from former *Patriot* crew member John McFarlane of Georgetown, South Carolina, to David A. Cumming dated April 6, 1813. It suggests the loss of the ship may have been an inside job or because of a loss if its commander. McFarlane said that many of the crew decided they would not go to sea with a Captain Merrihaw and suggested that Samuel Coon, the sailing master, may have taken over for the voyage. He said "four black prisoners" were used to return the ship to New York to its owners but not for use as a privateer.

The *Patriot* did not sail as a privateer on the voyage, for it is believed Governor Alston would never have agreed to let Theodosia travel this way. Oddly, however, it should be noted that she traveled without a companion. McFarlane was sure the ship went down, one way or the other. "I am doubtful from the length of time this vessel has been missing that there is but little hope of her being heard of," McFarlane wrote.[7]

There were many deathbed confessions from former pirates over the years. Two men tried and executed for other crimes, Jean DeFarges and Robert Johnson, were among them. An 1820 story in the *New York Advertiser* claimed the two men had been crew members on the *Patriot*, led a mutiny, scuttled the ship, and killed all the men on board. In 1878, the *New York Times* ran a story that included a confession from Benjamin F. Burdick, who was on his deathbed in Michigan and confessed to a minister's wife that he had been on the pirate ship that took the *Patriot*. Burdick claimed that Theodosia changed into white garments and carried a Bible in her hand as she walked the plank. There were severe storms off the coast of the Outer Banks at the time the *Patriot* disappeared and several ships on the same route were damaged. Legends claim that Theodosia haunts her plantation, the Oaks; the North Carolina Outer Banks; Richmond Hill (Burr's home in present-day Greenwich Village, New York); and Bald Head Island.[8]

*

14. Legacy of Legends and Lies

Judge Walter Clark mentioned the Theodosia Burr Alston legend in his remarks at the dedication of the statue to Burns during the ceremony when it was dedicated in Burnsville. He called any association of Burns to her demise was a "remarkable mis-statement in regard to a man whose actions had been so distinguished." He said that the *Patriot* may have been lost in a gale and not to pirates and that it was an "outrageous and absurd insult to one of the most gallant men North Carolina has ever produced."[9]

*

Major Graham Daves and Dr. J.W. Sanders, a former senator from Carteret County, both wrote letters that were printed in several newspapers to "set the record straight" that Burns had nothing to do with the demise of Theodosia Burr Alston.

A letter to the editor of the *Daily Journal* in New Bern in the December 14, 1895, issue may have been what started the myth about Burns being involved in the death of Theodosia Burr Alston. R.W. Humphrey wrote that a Mrs. Wescott on Roanoke Island claimed to have many relics from the *Patriot*, many of which were purported to belong to Alston. Humphrey suggests they ought to be exhibited at the New Bern Fair.

Humphrey says that Alston met her fate at the hands of "the pirate Ottaway Burns and his piratical crew off Roanoke Island." He said that Wescott was "resting on the beach hills" when the *Patriot* came ashore and was the first to board the ship. She claimed a breakfast table was set and "unmolested" and that many pictures and silk dresses belonging to Alston were on the cabin floor.[10] This account does not say what became of the ghost ship after that.

*

At least one account of the story earlier in this book when Burns had to go ashore to retrieve one-third of his crew that had gotten drunk at an island "pothouse" and refused to leave goes against

Captain Otway Burns

reality as well. It reported that Burns killed the group's leader, but that is not true. No one died in the incident.

*

One easily refuted legend involves Burns' crew and another famous ship, HMS *Bounty*.

It's been written that some of the crew of the last voyage of the *Snap Dragon* who were captured and sent to Dartmoor prison were later forced to sail with Captain William Bligh and participated in the mutiny led by Lieutenant Fletcher Christian. Supposedly, they were later put ashore in the South Seas on Pitcairn Island.[11] The only problem is that the mutiny occurred in 1789, long before the last voyage of the *Snap Dragon*. Burns was 14 that year.

• • •

The Swansboro Area Heritage Center documents that crew member James Chadwick once fell overboard on one of the *Snap Dragon* voyages and that Burns jumped in the ocean to save him.

*

Swansboro High School, which looks right down on Queens Creek in the area where Burns grew up, is nicknamed the Pirates. "It's in his honor," said Carteret County historian Dee Lewis, "but he wouldn't like the name."

Lewis shared a legend about Burns' death.

"There is a story that his body was unceremoniously dropped on the dock at Beaufort shortly after his death, and the men that brought him over from Portsmouth said, 'Here's your hero' [obviously with sarcasm]," Lewis said. It has been written in more than one source that Burns' body was dropped "unboxed" on the wharf at Beaufort.[12]

Lewis said that generations of people were named Otway or Burns and that history has treated the old privateer with respect.

14. Legacy of Legends and Lies

"He's well regarded," Lewis said. There are also plenty of folks who claim to be kin to Burns.

Burns, like most historical figures, has to be remembered as a human, Lewis said. For a descendant, Lewis is pretty even-handed in his assessment of the captain.

"He had good and bad traits. I admire him," Lewis said. "He was an important man with character flaws. On his ship, he was judge, jury, and executioner. I suspect he was a bit of a bully, a braggart, a tough guy. A colleague of mine [looking at the portrait] once said, 'He's got weasel eyes.' But his stands in the legislature, when the western part of North Carolina was underrepresented—he took steps to correct that and a lot of people hated him for it, but he had a good sense of fairness."

Lewis also said that Burns' ego took a beating over time and that life as a legend came at a price.

"He was famous after the war and still young. He was not going to be that famous again."

◆ ◆ ◆

Lewis also has some theories into the personal problems Burns had with his first wife Joanna.

"He was an alpha male. I suspect he abused his wife. She moved in with her older sister, Experience Grant Dixon. Him being unwilling to pay her debts is strange. Him being gone all the time didn't help and can you turn that [aggression] off when you go home?" Lewis said.

The historian added that Experience lived between Stella and Maysville, about 20 miles away, so it would not have been easy for Burns to see Owen when he was in port. Father and son were not close in Owen's formative years and it presented a challenge when Otway finally got custody.

"When he went to get Owen, Owen didn't want to go," Lewis said. "He didn't really know Otway. Otway's second wife was very well to do, but Owen did not have a good relationship with her."

Captain Otway Burns

◆ ◆ ◆

Author Jack Robinson mentions in his research the origins of the *Snap Dragon* should be in question. He says he found a report that the ship was originally the *Zephyr*, but its measurements don't match. He also said nothing resembling the name *Levere* was on the New York Register according to Howard I. Chappelle, who wrote *In Search for Speed Under Sail*.

◆ ◆ ◆

Storyteller Rodney Kemp of the Beaufort area said that Burns "outlived his usefulness" to describe the final 20 years of Burns' life.

◆ ◆ ◆

There are plenty of stories about how Burns spent his last days drinking, quarreling, and fighting with all comers in the taverns of Portsmouth Island. There are reports that he would dress in his old captain's uniform before setting out on a hell-raising expedition.

◆ ◆ ◆

A mother who lives on Harker's Island, in Carteret County not far from Beaufort, said that it is not unusual to be in a Parent-Teacher Association meeting at her children's school and, when something difficult arises, hear someone say, "Are we going to have to go all Otway on someone?"

◆ ◆ ◆

Burns' first biographer, John H. Bryan, worried that because of his end of life, the captain's legacy would be lost to history. In his essay from 1855, "Otway Burns and the Snap Dragon," he wrote, "From my earliest childhood, the adventures of the Snap Dragon, when commanded by Otway Burns, have been rehearsed in my hearing by old tars, many of whom are now dead and in a few years

14. Legacy of Legends and Lies

perhaps Otway Burns and the Snap Dragon will be looked upon as never having had any existence."[13]

Bryan may have been prescient. Burns does not appear in many histories, and when he does, the information is often inaccurate. Not many outside of the Carteret County region know anything about him.

◆ ◆ ◆

Respected historian Lindley S. Butler said that Kemp Battle's work and Clark's commentary at the statue dedication were "heavily mythologized and error filled."[14] But he does give Burns his due, writing that the "consensus on his iron will, courage, endurance, self-confidence, direct manner, forceful personality, decisive and creative leadership, mastery of seamanship, and colorful character" created a "larger than life individual who deserves his niche in the pantheon of North Carolina heroes."[15]

Statue of Otway Burns in Burnsville, North Carolina (courtesy State Archives of North Carolina).

◆ ◆ ◆

Captain Otway Burns

That there are rumors and suggestions that Burns fathered other children are not unexpected. However, the only record that exists listing him as a father is for Owen, who was born in 1810.

Owen may not have been close with his father at an early age, but he certainly followed in his footsteps. He was a midshipman by the time he was 14 and was promoted to master of the *John Adams* in 1831. He was in the Mediterranean Squadron 0 as a first lieutenant. He served in the U.S. Navy from April 8, 1834, until he resigned in 1840. His last service was three years in the Pacific on the man-of-war USS *Falmouth*.

Owen, at 39, married Martha Armstrong of Baltimore, at 15, on November 18, 1849. She was the daughter of Solomon Armstrong and granddaughter of General John Armstrong. He and Martha had nine children: I.R., Eugene, Richard, Jerome, Charles O., Walter Francis, Edwin Oscar, Owen Jr., and Lillian.

There is an unsourced, unverified story that Owen operated a blockade runner for the Confederacy during the Civil War, bringing supplies into North Carolina. He was allegedly captured off the coast of Florida and sent to a POW camp where his health suffered. The legend goes that Martha walked from Fredericktown, Maryland, to Washington, D.C., to personally obtain a pardon from Abraham Lincoln.

There was a rumor that Owen had a half sister named Harriet Hall Burns from the marriage of Otway and Jane Hall. Harriet lived from 1827 to 1882 and married Richard Canady in 1844. The story goes that Owen hated her so much that Otway had her live with the Canady family in Onslow County, which is how she met her husband. Descendants deny she was Otway's daughter.[16] Owen died in 1869.

◆ ◆ ◆

It is difficult when researching Otway Burns to sort out fact from fiction—that's been well established in this book. One thing that makes it so difficult is the fact that "credible sources" got so

14. Legacy of Legends and Lies

many things wrong over the years, combining blatant inaccuracies with truthful information in a believable way.

For example, the *Goldsboro Messenger* ran "A Scrap of Carolina History" in its Monday, July 13, 1874, edition, citing the *Charlotte Observer*'s correspondence from Beaufort as a "morceau of State history." The piece is accurate for the first quarter, saying of the *Snap Dragon*, "The fleetness of the vessel, the skill and nautical knowledge which he displayed, and his boldness and daring, backed by a gallant crew, soon made the name of 'Otway Burns' a terror to all British men in American waters."[17] However, the story then mentions that Burns had an observatory on top of his Beaufort home where he used a spyglass to constantly scan the ocean. He didn't move to Beaufort until after the war. "Whenever he would discover a ship sailing under the British colors, he would hurry to the 'Snap Dragon,' which he always kept in a state of readiness for seagoing, and put off in pursuit of him." Of course, that's not how privateering worked. The story then says that because Burns did so much damage to British shipping that the "British Council" met to figure out a way to capture him and built a special ship with an experienced captain specifically to go after Burns. To add to the tall tale, the story continues that the British ship disguised itself and was able to capture the *Snap Dragon* without firing a shot, turning out to be a "terrible man-of-war, bristling with cannons and guns in the hands of warriors. Burns was compelled to give up." It says he was released from British custody after the War of 1812 ended. Not only is the piece wildly inaccurate about the end of the *Snap Dragon*, the dates, and locations, but it is also simply ridiculous to repeat a story that privateering could be conducted from a captain's home, where he stared at the horizon all day, waiting for prize ships to come into view, hustling to the dock, convening his crew, and then being able to run them down with a sailing craft—it's more Disney animated story.

The same story describes Burns as a "short, thick set, red faced man, of a jovial disposition, and very fiery and passionate ... towards the end of his life he became very dissipated [*sic*; it means 'given to sensual pleasures']."

*

Burns was a Mason. Governor David Swain was interested in Burns and once delivered a lecture on him and got Burns' death year incorrect.[18]

◆ ◆ ◆

A story in the form of a pamphlet titled, "Remarks During a Residence—from June 18th to August 11th, 1820, at the Cape of Good Hope, by Thomas George Love" published in Buenos Aires, told of another seafaring legend. The story appeared in the *Newbern Sentinel* on Saturday, April 19, 1828, and the author recalls a tale but writes he cannot remember the name of the teller.

According to the story, a successful American privateer captured a British merchant ship near the Cape of Good Hope and the captain boarded the ship to take possession. The author of the pamphlet recalls that the privateer was named *Rambler* but that the master was Burns. Upon boarding the ship, the captain immediately saw a beautiful woman on deck in tears. He was allegedly so taken back that he offered comfort to the woman by stating that "he had only boarded to hear the news, and have the pleasure of a glass of wine with the captain." She was the wife of the captain, and after meeting with the ship's commander, the privateer told her husband that despite the fact he could lawfully claim the ship as a prize, seeing the wife in distress was too much. Instead, he took paper and pen and "made over all claim on the vessel to the fair creature that had so interested him." Adding to the grandeur of the story, the privateer shortly made his way into Table Bay, and the story of his generosity had apparently preceded him, causing a British ship to not only decline to attack his ship but instead have its band strike up "Yankee Doodle" as a tribute as the ship passed by. It also states that the woman was pregnant at the time and, once in port, delivered

14. Legacy of Legends and Lies

her baby and named him after the privateersman. "Privateersmen are generally reputed to be so hard hearted and mercenary, that one would hardly believe this detail. Yet it is well authenticated at the Cape and I feel the greatest pleasure in relating it. I had the happiness of knowing the individual whose conduct was at once so delicate and humane. The person of whom this honorable anecdote is told, was Captain OTWAY BURNS, of Beaufort, N. Carolina."[19]

* * *

The *Wilmington Journal* of Friday, July 17, 1874, ran a story about Burns that repeats the myth of his running his privateering operation from the top floor of his postwar home and adds a twist. It relates that the British Council met twice to try to figure out how to catch Burns and built a ship specifically to catch him and put an experienced (but unnamed) captain in charge. The story said that the ship found him in South America and, after disguising itself as a merchantman, captured Burns and the *Snap Dragon* without firing a shot. The "fake news" continued that Burns went to prison for the duration of the war and was "poor for the rest of his days."

* * *

Despite his exploits and fame in several arenas, Burns had faded into obscurity by the time of his death. John Hill Wheeler, who wrote the first popular history of the state called *Historical Sketches of North Carolina from 1584 to 1851*, did not even mention the captain. Burns didn't make the history books until Wheeler's *Reminiscences and Memoirs of North Carolina and Eminent North Carolinians* was published posthumously over 30 years later.[20] It's likely that he only made the cut then because a narrative of the log of *Snap Dragon* cruises of 1812 and 1813 had been published in the *North Carolina University Magazine* in 1855 and 1856.

Otway's grandson Walter F. Burns, who was an investment banker in New York and Chicago, set out in the latter half of the century to make sure his grandfather did not disappear from history and to rehabilitate his image. The family had a portrait copied from an 1815 painting, erected a grave monument with the cannon on top in Beaufort, and saw a bronze statue of Burns installed in Burnsville. Walter also penned a biography of Otway. There were public addresses given at these dedications by historian Kemp P. Battle and Chief Justice Walter Clark (who added to the state's records by compiling North Carolina Civil War regimental histories), but their remarks were full of myths and inaccuracies, which unfortunately, like the earlier history of the *Prometheus*, were used as the basis for much research, muddying an era that was aging quickly.

* * *

Former newspaperwoman Ruth Barbour wrote an account of how the *Snap Dragon* got its name in her entertaining historical novel *The Cruise of the* Snap Dragon, published in 1976. So much info in this book is true that at times it is hard to separate fact from fiction. Her account, which I couldn't corroborate with any other source, says the ship's name, *Snap Dragon*, was inspired by a tavern game of the same name played one afternoon by Otway and several of his potential investors and friends. Snapdragon or flapdragon was a game that became popular in Victorian times. The "dragon" was a dish filled with raisins (sometimes other candied fruit) and brandy or some other alcoholic beverage, which was then set on fire. Participants then snap their fingers or use a spoon to flip the flaming fruit into the air and then catch them with their mouths. It was often played around Christmas, often with the lights turned down or off and with salt added to the fire to give it an eerie glow. It was mentioned by Shakespeare as "flap-dragon" and also appeared in the works of Charles Dickens and Lewis Carroll, and was put into Samuel Johnson's dictionary in 1755. In Robert Chambers' *Book of Days*, published in 1864, there was even a ditty to go with the game:

> Here he comes with flaming bowl,
> Don't he mean to take his toll,
> Snip! Snap! Dragon!

14. Legacy of Legends and Lies

Otway Burns grave marker dedication in Beaufort, North Carolina (courtesy State Archives of North Carolina).

> Take care you don't take too much,
> Be not greedy in your clutch,
> Snip! Snap! Dragon!
>
> With his blue and lapping tongue
> Many of you will be stung,
> Snip! Snap! Dragon!
>
> For he snaps at all that comes
> Snatching at his feast of plums,
> Snip! Snap! Dragon!
>
> But Old Christmas makes him come,
> Though he looks so fee! fa! fum!
> Snip! Snap! Dragon!
>
> Don't 'ee fear him but be bold—
> Out he goes his flames are cold,
> Snip! Snap! Dragon![21]

*

Captain Otway Burns

Even though Judge Clark's speech at the grave dedication in Beaufort in 1901 might have contained plenty of factual errors, he did sum up the life of Otway Burns quite eloquently: "In the sea's wildest mood he was its master and rode on its crest to fame and fortune."[22]

Epilogue

THE ORIGINAL *SNAP DRAGON* LOGS are gone. The official copies are believed to have been burned when the British sacked Washington, D.C. However, portions were published in the *Carolina Federal Republican* in New Bern on September 18, 1813, the *Raleigh Register* and *North Carolina Gazette* on September 24, 1813, and the *New Berne Weekly Journal* on February 27, 1896, in addition to the reprints in 1855 and 1856 in the *North Carolina University Magazine*.

*

Technically, the United States is the only maritime power that reserved the right to employ privateers throughout the 19th century, having declined to sign the 1856 Treaty of Paris. The United States has not commissioned any privateers since the War of 1812, but the Confederate States employed them. Although they didn't use privateers, commerce raiding was effective for Germany during World War I. America outlawed privateering in 1907 by adhering to the terms of the Second Hague Conference. Spain followed suit the next year.

*

The Declaration of Paris in 1856 pretty much marked the end of the privateering profession. A provision to make private property exempt from seizure was proposed by the United States, which ironically never took action on the declaration. The proposal was made again at the peace conference at The Hague in 1899.

*

Epilogue

The Confederate States of America issued letters of marque on April 17, 1861, with instructions for privateers to "burn, sink, destroy."[1]

*

On March 6, 1834, John "Yellow Jacket John" Bailey conveyed 100 acres of land to the state of North Carolina for the establishment of a town in Yancey County that would be called Burnsville. Not only was the town of Burnsville named for Otway, but officials there put up a statue in his honor on July 5, 1909. More than 4,000 people attended the ceremony where several notable speakers took the stage.[2] The *Twin-City Daily Sentinel* of Winston-Salem wrote that the plaza and courthouse "is enlivened by his statue in bronze, with cocked-hat and speaking trumpet and a most nautical air. It is in all the Appalachians the only thing which even hints of the sea."[3] The *Asheville Citizen* reported there was a dance in Beaufort at the Atlantic Hotel to celebrate the Burnsville monument and that several women fainted during the 96-degree day in the ceremony attended by 1,500. A portrait of Burns painted by noted New York artist William M. Chase was also presented. A number of Masons were on hand to consecrate the cornerstone of the monument, which was made from gray granite from Mount Airy, North Carolina. The bronze statue was produced in Florence, Italy.[4]

Burns was the first North Carolinian honored with an individual statue outside of Raleigh. The captain would appreciate that Burnsville is the highest county seat above sea level east of the Rockies. At the dedication, Judge Walter Clark, a noted dignitary and author of several Confederate regimental histories, was the keynote speaker. Clark, chief justice of the North Carolina Supreme Court, said in his remarks that Burns was "a terror to the British merchant marine."[5]

The inscription on the plaque of the statue reads:

OTWAY BURNS
BORN IN ONSLOW COUNTY

Epilogue

N.C. 1775.
DIED AT PORTSMOUTH
N.C. 1850.
SAILOR–SOLDIER–STATESMAN.
NORTH CAROLINA'S FOREMOST SON
IN THE WAR OF 1812–15.
FOR HIM, THIS TOWN IS NAMED.
HE GUARDED WELL OUR SEAS,
LET OUR MOUNTAINS HONOR HIM.

In 1983, the town of Swansboro also erected a statue in Burns' honor. It is located in Bicentennial Park on the town's White Oak River waterfront near the North Carolina Highway 24 bridge and stands 12 feet tall. Burns is portrayed in a military uniform with a rolled-up document in one hand and pointing toward Queen's Creek. The inscription reads:

CAPT. OTWAY BURNS, JR. 1775–1850

PRIVATEER, LEGISLATOR, SHIPBUILDER AND MERCHANT. BORN 2 MILES FROM HERE ON QUEEN'S CREEK. COMMANDER OF THE "SNAPDRAGON" AND A HERO IN THE WAR OF 1812.
BUILT STEAMBOAT "PROMETHEUS" HERE IN 1818. CAST THE DECIDING VOTE FOR CONSTITUTIONAL CONVENTION OF 1835 INTERRED IN OLD BURYING GROUND BEAUFORT.

*

In addition to the statues, there were two naval destroyers named after Burns. The USS *Burns* DD-171 was launched in 1918 from the San Francisco Navy Yard and served in World War I. The USS *Burns* DD-588 was built at the Charleston Navy Yard, going into World War II service in 1942 and serving in almost every major operation in the Pacific theater from Wake Island to the Japanese surrender in 1945. For a short time after the war, the ship's bell from the DD-588 was on display at the Burnsville statue. The statue was vandalized a few times over the years, separating some of the elements.

Epilogue

USS *Burns*, underway circa 1922–1924 (Naval History and Heritage Command).

*

There is an Otway Burns chapter of the Daughters of the American Revolution, a Snap Dragon chapter of the Daughters of the War of 1812, and an Otway Burns chapter Sea Scouts. In 1917, a group of young men from Carteret County who enlisted in the army were known as the Otway Burns Boys, as was a group of World War II navy pilots. According to the Swansboro Area Heritage Center, there was the Captain Otway Burns Byway on Ocracoke Island. There have been countless restaurants, hotels, and other items that carried or carry the name Otway Burns or Snap Dragon.

*

In 1941, editor Aycock Brown of the *Beaufort News* tried to lobby for the new Marine Corps base being built in Onslow County to be named after Burns. North Carolina's Josephus Daniels had been

Epilogue

secretary of the navy when Brown started his efforts, so he thought he had a real chance. Daniels was appointed ambassador to Mexico, and the effort fizzled; the new base was named Marine Barracks, New River instead.[6]

A portrait commissioned by Burns' grandson Walker Francis Burns of New York was presented to the North Carolina House of Representatives in 1901. It was painted by F. Mahler, a pupil of William Merritt Chase, and shows Burns around age 40. The Swansboro Area Heritage Center notes in its records that there was a revival of interest in the 1890s in genealogy and that families wanted to show connections to America's past and that this was when Walter Francis Burns, a successful New York banker, became motivated to restore his grandfather's legacy.

*

It was said that one of Otway's cannons was used as a marker to separate Old Town and New Town in Beaufort and that a marker replaced the cannon when the cannon was removed and placed on Burns' grave marker on July 24, 1901.

*

The community of Otway in Carteret County is named for Burns. It is eight miles east of Beaufort on Highway 70. Both sections in the straits area wanted to be called Otway on the east side of Ward's Creek. It finally broke into two sections, one named Otway and the other Bettie.

*

A good bit of my time was spent in libraries and online studying records. Perhaps the most entertaining day of research was spent talking with three men at the Carteret County History Museum. Rodney Kemp and Bob Guthrie are retired schoolteachers and Durward "Dee" Lewis worked years in lawn maintenance and as a

Epilogue

bread truck delivery driver. All three men study history and genealogy of the area and are fans of Otway Burns. Lewis spends a lot of his time researching and compiling local genealogies.

At this point, I should mention that these men are part of a group called the Fish House Liars that meet regularly to share yarns and sometimes food and drink. Or at least they were; they told me that Lewis was kicked out of the club because he would only tell true stories. As Kemp told me—a line he said he stole—"everything I tell you is true, except the parts that are not."

The men shared a story about how Otway was able to finance his privateer and also name his ship during a tavern visit in New Bern. Kemp, a natural storyteller who regularly makes local history presentations with Burns as a frequent subject, tells the story best, following close to the account in Barbour's novel:

> He was at the tavern with some monied men and he was not having success. So the men ordered a pot of boiling rum with raisins. They played a game where the object was to flip raisins out of the pot with a spin and catch them out of the air in the mouth without spilling them. No man could do it except Burns, who caught them all. The men were so impressed with his skill [and pain tolerance] they decided to invest with him. And the name of the game? It was called Snap Dragon.

Kemp said he believed the story in Ruth Barbour's *Cruise of the Snap Dragon* was a true one. I asked if it was a novel, then wasn't her story fiction? All three of the men insisted that Barbour had been a by-the-book journalist "who wouldn't tell a lie" and that she only called it a novel because she didn't have documentation for everything.

*

There were conflicting findings early in my research that the steamboat *Prometheus* was built in Beaufort. This may be because Burns owned property there, including a shipyard. It's also because an early account of local history by James Sprunt called *Chronicles*

Epilogue

of the Cape Fear River indicated this and many subsequent histories used this as source material. Sprunt based his work on the account of "witness" Colonel J.G. Burr.[7] However, numerous newspaper accounts of the day during the construction of the launch show that the ship was built and launched in Swansboro. Burns did not sell his Swansboro shipyard until 1819. The *Raleigh Minerva* of April 17, 1818, referenced the ship being built in Swansboro, as did a June 27, 1818, story in the *New Bern Sentinel*. The *Daily National Intelligencer* in Washington, D.C., reported on June 22, 1818, that the ship had arrived in Wilmington from Swansboro.

*

Many historians describe the *Prometheus* as a side wheeler, but illustrations show it as a stern wheeler.[8]

*

Author Kemp Battle wrote that Burns was "a privateer in time of war, and a most useful legislator for his state in time of peace."[9]

*

Naval historian Edward Stanton Maclay compared Burns to John Paul Jones. Maclay wrote in 1916 that Burns captured 42 prizes with a value of $4 million, had combat with several men-of-war, took over 300 POWs, and had "a record of astounding audacity and brilliant success that has few parallels."[10] Burns was unusual in that he often restored private property and personal investments among his captured cargo and tried to avoid men-of-war when possible.

*

Writer Tucker Littleton pointed out that in mythology, Prometheus angered Zeus because he befriended man. That seems to be an irony of Burns' legislative career as he was essentially run out of office for voting for issues that would benefit all the people of the state. Burns wasn't being clever or dramatic with the name

Epilogue

regarding his life at that point, as the steamship was built years before he entered politics, but it certainly adds to the captain's mystique.

*

The last veteran of the War of 1812, Hiram Cronk, died in 1905 in New York.[11] The last person to draw a pension for that war—the daughter of a veteran—died in 1946.

*

There were 20,000 POWs in British prisons from the War of 1812, most of them privateers. Britain did not exchange them in an effort to discourage the practice.

*

Dartmoor was the most notorious British prison and remembered by prisoners "as miserable, unhealthy, seemingly endless, and—for many—deadly."[12] One thing peace negotiators neglected to settle was the release and return of American POWs after the war. In April 1815, after peace was agreed to, the prison superintendent imposed restrictions on rations, which angered the prisoners and they gathered to protest. The guards panicked and fired into the crowd of men, killing 7 and wounding over 30 more. Some accounts blame the incident on inexperienced guards, but many accounts by prisoners later on asserted that the attack was deliberate. Eventually, the British government apologized and compensated the families of the dead and wounded in what became known as the Dartmoor Massacre.

*

Many newspaper articles over the years after Burns' death retold inaccurate stories about his war experience. It was repeated several times that Burns was captured on the last voyage of the *Snap Dragon*

Epilogue

and spent the rest of the war in Dartmoor prison. He was not even on the ship at the time of the capture.

*

There isn't universal agreement about the cannon on Burns' tombstone in the Beaufort cemetery. Kemp, Guthrie, and Lewis told me that the cannon was one from the *Snap Dragon*. However, the ship was captured by the British, sold, and sank during a storm, so the gun would have had to have been removed before the fourth and final voyage. There are newspaper articles offering contradictory opinions, one saying it was a revolutionary-era gun. Guthrie said it was possible that both were true. The men said the cannon had been stuck in the ground and was used as a boundary marker separating Old Beaufort from New Beaufort and that many local realtors still use those terms. A black stake stands in place of the cannon now.

*

General Andrew Jackson used privateers under Jean Lafitte and slaves in his victory at the Battle of New Orleans. Slaves were promised freedom in exchange for their service during this desperate time, but when Jackson realized he'd gone too far, he reneged on that promise. He said that the slave owners had promised emancipation and changed their minds and he did not have the authority to take another man's property or the money to buy all the slaves' freedom. At least one pension for a Black soldier went to his master and the master's heirs.[13]

*

Lafitte played a key role for Jackson during the Battle of New Orleans and had a colorful career after the war, even working as a spy for Spain at one point. He disappeared in the 1820s, and it's been written that he was killed in a failed pirate attack or from a fever in Mexico. One of the most intriguing legends says that neither of those is true—that he retired to Lincolnton, North Carolina, near

Epilogue

Charlotte and spent the rest of his days there. A man by the name of Lorenzo Ferrier moved to the town and led a quiet life but often told pirate stories to groups of children. Ferrier met a man who was part of another legend: he was Napoleon's Field Marshal Peter Ney and had escaped a firing squad in Europe to live out his days in North Carolina. It was said the two men had an angry exchange. When Union troops approached Lincolnton during the Civil War, Ferrier got a local man to help him hide one of his "treasure chests" and paid the man with a handful of gold coins and a gold watch. Others have speculated that the man was not Lafitte but one of his captains.[14]

*

There are conflicting stories about the bricks at Fort Macon, including one that states Burns and Manney were bitter competitors. This seems to contradict the fact that they wrote a letter together for the newspapers, pleading their cases as reliable vendors with a good product. Like many things in history, some of the exact details are confusing and answers were hard to come by. Why did the relationship between the contractors and the army engineers take what appeared to be such a hard turn and quick deterioration? What caused the relationship that seemed fine enough in public in 1827 to turn so sharply two years later? Even though all of these events were chronicled in documents and newspapers, a clear picture of how it exactly transpired is not available.

Fort Macon is a popular tourist stop now and was a prime location for beach visitors for picnics and social events in the 19th century. It has stood the test of time for sure. By 1860, it was in poor condition and was used as a prison after the Civil War. It was abandoned after 1880 but then put back into use during the Spanish-American War. It was once again abandoned after that conflict. Between 1900 and 1924, the guns were dismantled and sold. The U.S. government wanted to close it and the state of North Carolina wanted to buy it but didn't have the money. Through the work of a congressman and senator, the federal government ended

Epilogue

up giving the property to the state, and it became a state park in 1924. From 1934 to 1935, the Civilian Conservation Corps did some work on it. The fort was once again put back into military use when the federal government leased it from 1942 until April 1, 1945. On October 1, 1946, it returned to the North Carolina state park system.[15]

*

The Fish House Liars also told me a great story about the Odd Fellows Lodge on Turner Street in Beaufort. The masons who were working on Fort Macon were members of the lodge and, according to the men, were taking home bricks each night from the job and then working by torchlight on their new building. Since these were U.S. government bricks, they were eventually caught and told to stop; however, the workers were told they could have any of the bricks that were broken during the day. So the masons made sure a sufficient number were cracked at the end of their shift. The lodge, like the fort, still stands today.

*

Many of Burns' former crew members lived on the eastern shore of the North River and Ward's Creek in the Beaufort area, and that's how the community came to be named Otway, Kemp said—out of respect for their old commander. But why the captain's first name?

"Because we knew him better—that's what they'd say," Kemp said. "If a place was named for someone and they used the first name, it meant that person [being honored] was one of them."

The men gave the example of Harkers Island (Ebenezer Harker of Boston), Morehead City (Governor John Motley Morehead of Rockingham, North Carolina), Marshallberg, and Salter (formerly Salter's) Path being last names of people "not from there." There are other places called Bettie, Stacy, and Stella. Bettie was named for a schoolteacher from Salter Path who ran the post office from her home and people would say, "Take this mail to Bettie."

Epilogue

The Oddfellows Lodge in Beaufort, North Carolina, allegedly built with "broken bricks" from Fort Macon (courtesy Kristi P. Brantley).

Kemp said he didn't know how Stella and Stacy were named but that he'd made up a couple of pretty good stories about them.

*

Kemp shared a poem titled, "The Saga of Otway Burns," by the late Carol Wylie Taylor that has made the rounds and that he uses in his presentations. It mentions the story surrounding the naming of the *Snap Dragon*, Burns' war heroics, Fort Macon, Burns' steamship,

Epilogue

and his grave marker. It even suggests his spirit might still be hanging around the area and checks another box of whether someone is a legend—do they have at least one poem written about them?

*

The *Hero*, the other lesser-known privateer that operated out of New Bern, captured five ships loaded with sugar and molasses valued at $20,000 during the war.[16]

*

William Shepard, whose home was called Shepard's Point and is today Morehead City, used his share of the *Snap Dragon* payoff to build the first steam-powered mill in New Bern on the Trent River, about one mile from the courthouse. It eventually closed due to increased competition.[17]

*

The dueling laws passed in North Carolina after the Stanley-Spaight duel stopped another group of participants close to Otway Burns. Captain Thomas A. Pasteur, a West Point graduate, was "a person of quarrelsome temper and disposition" who offered a challenge to Dr. James Manney, but Manney declined because of the severe consequences passed by the legislature for the survivor.[18] Pasteur went on to become a general.

*

Owen Burns, Otway's only son, served with distinction in the U.S. Navy. The June 2, 1827, *New Bern Sentinel* reported that he was serving as a midshipman on the USS *Constellation* under Commodore Charles G. Ridgeby.

*

There has been disagreement over the years about whether the *Snap Dragon* was originally the *Zephyr* or the *Levere*. Yet another

Epilogue

wrinkle exists in the shipbuilding records of the time: A Philadelphia customhouse document lists a schooner named the *Snap Dragon*, which was built at Smith's Creek, North Carolina, in 1806.[19] However, it is widely accepted that this was not the privateer.

*

In yet another twist over the origins of the *Snap Dragon*, a report in the *Beaufort News* of April 28, 1927, adds another turn. According to a report, "older citizens of Straits and Gloucester" said the privateer was built or refitted on the straits at what was the home of Ed Pigott, a Carteret County shipbuilder. They claimed that Burns and his men went into the local swamps and cut timber and that they made the sails on Pigott's porch.

*

In 1941, Mrs. Grayden Paul of Beaufort wrote a play about Otway Burns called *Unknown Seas*. It was produced in 1949 and played several times over the years.

*

Burns' desk was given to Duke University in 1929 and was eventually transferred to the North Carolina Maritime Museum in Beaufort, where it was on display at least until 2024. His sword is in the North Carolina Archives in Raleigh.

*

On hand for the Burnsville statue dedication was Burns' great-granddaughter Theodora Wilkins, who did the unveiling. J.K. Willis of New Bern created the monument and the program order went this way:

Opposite: **Otway Burns display at the North Carolina Maritime Museum in Beaufort, North Carolina, in 2024 (courtesy North Carolina Department of Natural and Cultural Resources).**

Epilogue

Grave marker with cannon from the *Snap Dragon* in the Old Burying Ground, Beaufort, North Carolina (courtesy Kristi P. Brantley).

Song: "America"
Prayer: Rev. Thomas P. Noe
Song: "Columbia, Gem of the Ocean"
Introduction of Speaker: Charles L. Abernathy, esq.
Oration: Judge William Clark
Unveiling: Theodora Wilkins
Salute: Newbern Naval Reserves
Benediction: Rev. Mr. Hornaday

*

Burns was laid to rest in the Old Burying Grounds of the Ann Street United Methodist Church in Beaufort, North Carolina. The inscription tells little of his story:

CAPT. OTWAY BURNS. / Son of Francis Burns. / Commander United States Privateer. / SNAP DRAGON / War 1812–15. / Born in Onslow County N.C. / 1775. / Died at Portsmouth N.C. / 1850. / BURNS.

Nautical and Shipping Terms

Aft, after: toward the stern of a ship

Bark: three-masted ship with square-rigged foremast and mainmast and fore-and-after rigged mizzenmast

Beam: width of a ship

Bowsprit: large spar extending over bow of ship from which jib sails are set

Brig: two-masted ship with square-rigged foremast and mainmast

Brigantine: two-masted ship with square-rigged foremast and mainmast, except for mainsail, which is fore-and-aft rigged

Bulwark: raised sides of a ship above the deck

Canister: shot made of small iron balls, giving a cannon a shotgun effect

Careen: lean ship on side for cleaning or repairs

Carronade: short, large caliber cannon for in-close fighting

Chaser: long gun used in a chase, usually mounted on bow or stern

Coaster: a shallow-hulled ship used for trading along the coast or region—not designed for ocean voyages. They can get into areas that deeper hulled ships cannot.

Cutting out: capture of a prize ship in port using small boats at night

Felucca: single- or two-masted, lateen-rigged vessel, popular with Spanish sailors

Forecastle: the forward part of the ship, usually forward of the foremast, below the upper deck and where the living quarters of the crew was typically located

Foremast: mast of ship nearest bow

Forward: in the direction of the bow

Nautical and Shipping Terms

Frigate: three-masted, fast, square-rigged ship with 24–50 guns

Grape: small iron balls in a canvas bag for use against personnel, much like canister

Helm: wheel used to control the rudder and steer the ship

Hogshead, often abbreviated hhds: a cask containing 63 gallons of wine or 64 gallons of beer

Hull down: when part of a ship is visible but the main part (hull) is not

Jib: a triangular sail set on bowsprit to the foremast

Leeward: the direction opposite from which the wind is blowing

Line: any rope not used to set sails

Lee, leeward: side of the ship or shore sheltered from the wind

Long boat: largest boat carried on ship for transporting supplies, cargo, and sometimes prisoners from ship to ship or ship to shore

Long Tom: a cannon with a long range, often used at the bow or stern

Lying to: stopping a boat/ship temporarily

Mainmast: second of ship with two or more masts

Man-of-war: heavily armed warship, could have up to 124 guns

Mizzenmast: mast closest to stern of a ship with three masts

Packet: passenger or mail boat that runs on a schedule between the same ports. They often carried mail, passengers, and some cargo and were usually fast.

Periauger: open work boat, usually with two masts and oars, common on North Carolina sounds and rivers

Port: left side of a ship or a harbor

Puncheon: a cask that holds 70–120 gallons

Quarterdeck: aft portion of deck, usually raised, command center

Schooner: ship with two or more masts fore- and aft-rigged

Scudding: to run before a gale/storm without the sails set on the vessel

Scupper: an opening in the side of a vessel that allowed water to drain

Ship of the line: multidecked battleship of 18th and 19th centuries with 74–100 guns

Sloop: single-masted ship that is fore- and aft-rigged, some with three masts, some with two masts

Nautical and Shipping Terms

Spanish Main: Spanish Florida and New Spain (what is now Texas, Mexico, all of Central America, to Colombia and Venezuela on the north coast of South America and including the ports of Veracruz, Porto Bello, Cartagena, and Maracaibo)

Spars: poles in a ship's rigging

Speaking horn or trumpet: a megaphone-type tube

Square-rigged: having the principal sails at right angles to the length of the ship, supported by horizontal yards attached to the mast(s)

Starboard: right side of a ship

Swivel gun: small cannon mounted on a swivel

Tack: a leg or portion of a trip sailed with the wind on one side of the ship, part of a series of straight runs that make a zigzag course

Tender: usually a supply ship for a man-of-war

Topsail: mast above the topmast

Virgin Islands: U.S.—St. Croix, St. John, and St. Thomas, sold to the United States by Denmark in 1917 for $25 million; British—Tortola, Virgin Gorda, Anegada, and Jost Van Dyke, to the east of Puerto Rico and the U.S. Virgin Islands, sometimes referred to as the Leeward Islands of the Lesser Antilles

Windward: side of the ship against which the wind is blowing.

Chapter Notes

Preface

1. Butler, Lindley S. "Otway Burns: A Legendary Privateer of the War of 1812," *Tributaries*, October 1998.

Chapter 1

1. Lawrence, R.C., "Captain Otway Burns," *The State*, August 30, 1941.
2. [attrib. John H. Bryan], "Otway Burns and the Snap Dragon," *North Carolina University Magazine*, 2nd. ser. 4 (1855): 407–13, 461–67.
3. Bryan, "Otway Burns and the Snap Dragon," *UNC Magazine* (referring to Burns's logbook), 1855, 408.

Chapter 2

1. Stephenson, Richard A., and William N. Still, Jr., eds., *The Submerged Cultural Resources of Swansboro, North Carolina*, 14.
2. Greene, Lucy, "Early History," 347.
3. Stephenson and Still, *Submerged Cultural Resources*, 16.
4. Stephenson and Still, *Submerged Cultural Resources*, 18.
5. Watson, Alan D., *Onslow County: A Brief History*, 51.
6. Greene, "Early History," 348.
7. Still, William N., Jr., and Richard Stephenson, "Shipbuilding and Boatbuilders in Swansboro 1800–1950."
8. Watson, *Onslow County*, 50.
9. Greene, "Early History," 350.
10. Lewis, Dee, interview.
11. Otway Burns Papers, July 6, 1809, Onslow County Clerk of Court and Register of Deeds.
12. Mobley, Joe A., ed., *The Way We Lived in North Carolina*, 47.
13. von Graffenried, Christoph, "Relation of My American Project," *Von Graffenreid's Account of the Founding of New Bern*, c. 1714.
14. Mobley, *The Way We Lived*, 182.
15. Jackson, Donald, and Dorothy Twohig, eds., *Diaries of George Washington*, Vol. 6, January 1790–December 1799, 112.
16. Watson, Alan D., *A History of New Bern and Craven County*, 110.
17. Watson, *History of New Bern*, 111.
18. Watson, *History of New Bern*, 122.
19. Hill, Mrs. Fred, ed., *Historic Carteret County, North Carolina 1663–1975*.

Chapter 3

1. "Neutrality Proclamation, 22 April 1793," *Founders Online*, National Archives.
2. Phalen, William, *The First War of the United States: The Quasi War with France 1798–1801*, 70–71.
3. Hickey, Donald R., *The War of 1812: A Forgotten Conflict*, 6.
4. Butler, Lindley S., "Otway Burns: A Legendary Privateer in the War of 1812," 8.
5. Hickey, *The War of 1812*, 11.
6. Hickey, *The War of 1812*, 29.
7. Hickey, *The War of 1812*, 5.
8. Lemmon, Sarah McCulloh, *North Carolina and the War of 1812*, 9.
9. Lemmon, *North Carolina and the War of 1812*, 14.

Chapter Notes

10. Watson, Alan D., *Onslow County: A Brief History*.
11. Lemmon, *North Carolina and the War of 1812*, 14.
12. Gardiner, Robert, ed., *The Naval War of 1812*.
13. Zimmerman, James Fulton, *Impressment of American Seamen*, 187.
14. Daughan, George C., *1812: The Navy's War*, 44–45.

Chapter 4

1. Coggeshall, George, *History of the American Privateers and Letters of Marque*, 5.
2. Dean, Jim, "Otway Burns and the Snap Dragon," *Wildlife in North Carolina*.
3. Good, Timothy S., *American Privateers of the War of 1812: The Vessels and Their Prizes as Recorded in* Niles' Weekly Register, 3.
4. Gardiner, Robert, ed., *The Naval War of 1812*, 29.
5. Maclay, Edgar Stanton, *A History of American Privateers*, viii.
6. Coggeshall, *History of the American Privateers*, 5.
7. Maclay, *A History of American Privateers*, 9.
8. Butler, Lindley S., "Otway Burns: A Legendary Privateer of the War of 1812," 9.
9. Butler, "Otway Burns," 10.
10. Watson, Alan D., *A History of New Bern and Craven County*.
11. Lemmon, Sarah McCulloh, *North Carolina and the War of 1812*, 23.
12. *Encyclopedia of the War of 1812*.
13. Chidsey, Donald Barr, *The American Privateers*, 44.
14. Maclay, *A History of American Privateers*, 9.
15. Chidsey, *The American Privateers*, 47.
16. Chidsey, *A History of American Privateers*, 47.
17. Chidsey, *A History of American Privateers*, 137.
18. Gilje, Paul A., "The End of the War: The Dartmoor Massacre and a Tainted Place," *Commonplace: The Journal of American Life*, Vol. 12, No. 4 (July 2012), www.commonplace.online.
19. Gilje, "The End of the War."
20. Coggeshall, *History of the American Privateers*, 1.
21. Good, *American Privateers of the War of 1812*, 3.
22. Good, *American Privateers of the War of 1812*, 177.
23. Good, *American Privateers of the War of 1812*, 88.
24. Hill, Mrs. Fred, ed., *Historic Carteret County, North Carolina 1663–1975*.
25. Butler, "Otway Burns," 10.

Chapter 5

1. Maclay, Edgar Stanton, "The Exploits of Otway Burns, Privateersman and Statesman," 875.
2. Maclay, "The Exploits of Otway Burns," 876.
3. Butler, Lindley S., "Otway Burns: A Legendary Privateer of the War of 1812," 10.
4. Hill, Mrs. Fred, ed., *Historic Carteret County, North Carolina 1663–1975*.
5. Butler, "Otway Burns," 10.
6. Moore, Elizabeth, *Records of Craven County, Vol. I*.
7. Angley, Wilson, *An Historical Overview of Beaufort Inlet, Cape Lookout Area of North Carolina*.
8. Watson, Alan D., *A History of New Bern and Craven County*, 250.
9. Maclay, "The Exploits of Otway Burns," 877.
10. Lawrence, R.C., "Captain Otway Burns," *The State*, August 30, 1941.
11. Bryan, "Otway Burns and the Snap Dragon," *North Carolina University Magazine*, 1855.
12. Maclay, "The Exploits of Otway Burns," 878.
13. Burns, Walter F., *Captain Otway Burns: Patriot, Privateer and Legislator*.
14. Maclay, "The Exploits of Otway Burns," 878.

Chapter Notes

15. Robinson, Jack, *Otway Burns and His Ship the* Snap Dragon, 68.
16. Maclay, "The Exploits of Otway Burns," 879.
17. Butler, Lindley S., *Pirates, Privateers and Rebel Raiders*, 79.
18. W.F. Burns, *Captain Otway Burns*.
19. Bryan, "Otway Burns and the Snap Dragon."
20. Butler, *Pirates, Privateers and Rebel Raiders*.
21. Maclay, "The Exploits of Otway Burns," 884.
22. Maclay, "The Exploits of Otway Burns," 885.
23. Bryan, "Otway Burns and the Snap Dragon."
24. Maclay, "The Exploits of Otway Burns," 887.
25. Maclay, "The Exploits of Otway Burns," 888.
26. W.F. Burns, *Captain Otway Burns*.
27. Maclay, "The Exploits of Otway Burns," 889.
28. W.F. Burns, *Captain Otway Burns*, 150.
29. Bryan, "Otway Burns and the Snap Dragon."

Chapter 6

1. Hickey, Donald R., *The War of 1812: A Forgotten Conflict*, 157.
2. Hickey, *The War of 1812*, 76.
3. Hickey, *The War of 1812*, 90.
4. Lemmon, Sarah McCulloh, *North Carolina and the War of 1812*, 31.

Chapter 7

1. Maclay, Edgar Stanton, "The Exploits of Otway Burns, Privateersman and Statesman," 892.
2. Maclay, "The Exploits of Otway Burns," 892.
3. Maclay, "The Exploits of Otway Burns," 892.
4. Burns, Walter F., *Captain Otway Burns: Patriot, Privateer and Legislator*, 154.

5. Maclay, "The Exploits of Otway Burns," 895.
6. Maclay, "The Exploits of Otway Burns," 895.
7. Maclay, "The Exploits of Otway Burns," 896.
8. Lawrence, R.C., "Captain Otway Burns."
9. Bryan, "Otway Burns and the Snap Dragon," *North Carolina University Magazine*, 1855.
10. Butler, Lindley S., "Otway Burns: A Legendary Privateer of the War of 1812," *Tributaries*, October 1998.
11. Lawrence, "Captain Otway Burns."
12. Lawrence, "Captain Otway Burns."
13. Butler, "Otway Burns," 13.
14. Coggeshall, George, *History of the American Privateers and Letters of Marque*, 147.
15. "Notice," *The Carolina Federal Republican*, New Bern, NC, October 2, 1813.
16. "Notice."
17. Watson, Alan D., *A History of New Bern and Craven County*.
18. Maclay, "The Exploits of Otway Burns," 905.
19. Bryan, "Otway Burns and the Snap Dragon."
20. Bryan, "Otway Burns and the Snap Dragon."
21. *Ibid.*

Chapter 8

1. Bryan, "Otway Burns and the Snap Dragon," *North Carolina University Magazine*, 1855.

Chapter 9

1. Hickey, Donald R., *The War of 1812: A Forgotten Conflict*, 218.
2. Maclay, Edgar Stanton, "The Exploits of Otway Burns, Privateersman and Statesman," 905–906.
3. Butler, Lindley S., "Otway Burns: A Legendary Privateer of the War of 1812," 14.

4. Dean, Jim, "Otway Burns and the *Snap Dragon,*" *Wildlife in North Carolina,* 2.
5. Maclay, "The Exploits of Otway Burns," 909.
6. Burns, Walter F., *Captain Otway Burns: Patriot, Privateer and Legislator,* 98.
7. "Reminiscences of Privateering in the War '12," *The Newbernian* (New Bern, NC), November 14, 1874.
8. Butler, "Otway Burns," 12.

Chapter 10

1. Howard, Hugh, "Joshua Barney Against the British," Historynet.com.
2. Eden, Steven, "Commodore Barney at the Bladensburg Races," *Naval History Magazine,* Vol. 24, No. 5, October 2010.
3. Eden, Steven, "Commodore Barney at the Bladensburg Races."
4. "Joshua Barney," American Battlefield Trust.
5. Hickey, Donald R., *The War of 1812: A Forgotten Conflict,* 199.
6. Hickey, *The War of 1812,* 236.
7. Hickey, *The War of 1812,* 281.
8. Gardiner, Robert, ed., *The Naval War of 1812,* 167.
9. Daughan, George C., *1812: The Navy's War,* 328.
10. Zimmerman, James Fulton, *Impressment of American Seamen,* 220.
11. Zimmerman, *Impressment of American Seamen,* 260–268.
12. Daughan, *1812,* 328.

Chapter 11

1. Robinson, Jack, *Otway Burns and His Ship the* Snap Dragon, 98.
2. Hill, Mrs. Fred, ed., *Historic Carteret County, North Carolina 1663–1975.*
3. Lemmon, Sarah McCulloh, and Tucker Reed Littleton, "Otway Burns, Jr.," NCPedia.
4. Angley, Wilson, *An Historical Overview of Beaufort Inlet, Cape Lookout Area of North Carolina,* 3.

5. Still, William N., Jr., and Richard Stephenson, "Shipbuilding and Boatbuilders in Swansboro 1800–1950," 10.
6. Still and Stephenson, "Shipbuilding and Boatbuilders," 8.
7. Still and Stephenson, "Shipbuilding and Boatbuilders," 9.
8. Littleton, Tucker R., "North Carolina's First Steamboat," p. 8.
9. Littleton, "North Carolina's First Steamboat," 10.
10. Littleton, "North Carolina's First Steamboat," 10.
11. Robinson, *Otway Burns,* 110.
12. Bishop, Roann, "The Ups and Downs of a Seafaring Man," *NCPedia.*
13. Watson, Alan D., *Onslow County: A Brief History,* 51.
14. Still and Stephenson, "Shipbuilding and Boatbuilders," 9.
15. "Notice," *Newbern Sentinel* (New Bern, NC), October 10, 1818.
16. Brown, J., "United States of America, North-Carolina District. To the Marshal of the District, Greeting," *Newbern Sentinel* (New Bern, NC), September 18, 1819.
17. Still and Stephenson, "Shipbuilding and Boatbuilders," 111.
18. Robinson, *Otway Burns,* 114.
19. Lemmon and Littleton, "Otway Burns, Jr."
20. Burns, Otway, "Challenge Accepted," *Newbern Sentinel* (New Bern, NC), January 4, 1823.
21. "Died," *Raleigh Register,* June 27, 1823.
22. "Early June 2–3 Hurricane of 1825," North Carolina Shipwrecks, northcarolinashipwrecks.blogspot.com.
23. "Newbern, June 4," *Raleigh Register,* June 14, 1825.
24. "Newbern, June 4."
25. The Judiciary Act of 1801 reorganized the federal courts into six circuits, assigning North Carolina to the Fifth Circuit. It also split the state into three judicial districts: the Albermarle, Cape Fear, and Pamptico. In 1872, this was changed to two districts, Eastern and Western.

Chapter Notes

26. Daniel, Beverly, "Marshal's Sale," *Fayetteville Weekly Observer* (Fayetteville, NC), June 23, 1825.
27. "Elizabeth City (NC) Oct. 8," *Raleigh Register*, October 21, 1825.
28. Lewis, Durward, Interview, 2020.
29. Angley, *Historical Overview of Beaufort Inlet*, 33.
30. Branch, Paul, *Fort Macon*, 45.
31. Branch, *Fort Macon*, 45.
32. Branch, *Fort Macon*, 52.
33. "Dinner to Lieut. William A. Eliason," *New Bern Sentinel* (New Bern, NC), September 15, 1827.
34. Barry, Richard Schriver, "Fort Macon: Its History," 165.
35. Branch, "Fort Macon," 55.
36. "Engineer Orders," *New Bern Spectator*, October 24, 1829.
37. Robinson, *Otway Burns*, 118.
38. Robinson, *Fort Macon*, 119.
39. Barry, "Fort Macon," 166.
40. "Beaufort, Sept. 3, 1833," *The Newbernian* (New Bern, NC), February 24, 1837.

Chapter 12

1. Butler, Lindley S., *Pirates, Privateers, and Rebel Raiders*, 91.
2. Watson, Alan, *Internal Improvements in Antebellum North Carolina*.
3. Watson, *Internal Improvements*.
4. Lawrence, R.C., "Captain Otway Burns," *The State*, August 30, 1941, 12.
5. Williams, Wiley J., "Rip Van Winkle State," *NCPedia*.
6. "Laws of N. Carolina Passed in 1827–28," *North Carolina Star*, February 14, 1828.
7. "General Assembly, House of Commons," *Raleigh Register*, January 9, 1829.
8. Burns, Otway, "Communications," *New Bern Sentinel* (New Bern, NC), December 7, 1831.
9. "Summary," *The Harbinger* (Chapel Hill, NC), January 23, 1834.
10. "Address," *Semi-Weekly Standard* (Raleigh, NC), April 21, 1860.
11. "Address."
12. Swain, David L., "Proclamation, by the Governor of N. Carolina," *Fayetteville Weekly Observer* (Fayetteville, NC), February 19, 1833.
13. "Notice," *Newbern Sentinel* (New Bern, NC), February 16, 1822.
14. "State Legislature," *Weekly Raleigh Register*, December 9, 1834.
15. "Harbor of Beaufort," *Weekly Standard* (Raleigh, NC), December 26, 1834.
16. Butler, Lindley S., *Pirates, Privateers and Rebel Raiders*, 91.
17. Ashe, S.A., "Captain Ashe Writes of Difference of Taste," *News and Observer* (Raleigh, NC), August 16, 1903.

Chapter 13

1. Robinson, Jack, *Otway Burns and His Ship the* Snap Dragon, 141.
2. Lemmon, Sarah McCulloh, and Tucker Reed Littleton, "Otway Burns, Jr.," *NCPedia*.
3. "Maritime National Historic Landmarks: Lightships," National Park Service.
4. Lemmon and Littleton, "Otway Burns, Jr."
5. "Proscription," *Fayetteville Weekly Observer* (Fayetteville, NC), July 16, 1845.
6. Burke, Kenneth E., Jr., *The History of Portsmouth North Carolina*.
7. Butler, Lindley S., *Pirates, Privateers and Rebel Raiders*, 92.
8. "The War Comes to Portsmouth," National Park Service.
9. U.S. Census, 1850.
10. "Overlooking the Sea in Eastern Carolina," *Twin-City Daily Sentinel* (Winston-Salem, NC), December 14, 1921.
11. "The Snap Dragon's Cannon," *Charlotte News*, February 7, 1901.
12. "Cannon on Pollock Street Not from Snap-Dragon, of Revolutionary Time," *Daily Journal* (New Bern, NC), February 8, 1901.
13. "Captain Otway Burns," *News and Observer* (Raleigh, NC), July 11, 1901.

Chapter Notes

Chapter 14

1. "A Suggestion for the Fair," R.W. Humphrey, letter to the editor, *Daily Journal* (New Bern, NC), December 14, 1895.
2. Meares, Hadley, "The Dramatic Life and Mysterious Death of Theodosia Burr," *Atlas Obscura*, March 9, 2022.
3. Meares, "The Dramatic Life."
4. Pool Family Papers, Outer Banks History Center, North Carolina Department of Natural and Cultural Resources.
5. "I'm Thinking," *Rocky Mount Telegram* (Rocky Mount, NC), September 13, 1952.
6. Pool Family Papers.
7. John McFarlane letter to David A. Cumming, April 6, 1813, South Caroliniana Library.
8. Meares, "The Dramatic Life."
9. "His Brave Deeds to Be Remembered," *News and Observer* (Raleigh, NC), July 25, 1901.
10. "A Suggestion for the Fair."
11. Paul, Mary, and Grayden Paul, *Folklore, Facts and Fiction About Carteret County in North Carolina Told in Story and Song*.
12. "Overlooking the Sea in Eastern Carolina," *Twin-City Daily Sentinel* (Winston-Salem, NC), December 14, 1921.
13. Bryan, "Otway Burns and the *Snap Dragon*."
14. Butler, Lindley S., *Pirates, Privateers and Rebel Raiders*, 75.
15. Butler, *Pirates, Privateers and Rebel Raiders*, 75.
16. Littleton, Tucker R., "A Brief Sketch of the Life and Exploits of Captain Otway Burns, Jr."
17. "A Scrap of History," *Goldsboro Messenger* (Goldsboro, NC), July 13, 1874.
18. "A Scrap of History."
19. "From the Baltimore American," *Newbern Sentinel* (New Bern, NC), April 19, 1828.
20. Butler, Lindley S., "Otway Burns: A Legendary Privateer of the War of 1812."
21. Chambers, Robert, *Book of Days*.
22. "Captain Otway Burns," *News and Observer* (Raleigh, NC), July 11, 1901.

Chapter 15

1. *Acts and Resolutions of the Second Session of the Provisional Congress of the Confederate States, Held at Montgomery, Ala* (Richmond: Enquirer Book and Job Press by Tyler, Wise, Allegre & Smith, 1861). Electronic edition, Documenting the American South, UNC-Chapel Hill, 19–20.
2. "Otway Burns Statue," *News and Observer* (Raleigh, NC), July 8, 1909.
3. "Overlooking the Sea in Eastern Carolina," *Twin-City Daily Sentinel* (Winston-Salem, NC), December 14, 1921.
4. "Erect Monument to Capt. Otway Burns," *Asheville Citizen*, June 28, 1909.
5. "Captain Otway Burns," *News and Observer* (Raleigh, NC), July 11, 1901.
6. "He Named Ship in Honor of Burns," *Beaufort News*, July 3, 1941.
7. Sprunt, James, *Chronicles of the Cape Fear River, 1660–1916*, East Carolina University Digital Collections, pp. 138–139, accessed December 18, 2023.
8. Littleton, Tucker R., "North Carolina's First Steamboat," *The State*, November 1977.
9. Burns, Walter F. *Captain Otway Burns: Patriot, Privateer and Legislator*, 71.
10. Maclay, Edgar Stanton, "The Exploits of Otway Burns, Privateersman and Statesman."
11. Bitzer, G.W., Camera, American Mutoscope and Biograph Company, and Paper Print Collection, *Funeral of Hiram Cronk* (United States: American Mutoscope and Biograph Company, 1905), video, https://www.loc.gov/item/00694398/.
12. "American Prisoners Watch as British Guards Fire into Their Ranks," https://www.nps.gov/articles/dartmoor-prison.htm.

Chapter Notes

13. "Blacks and the Battle of New Orleans: The Story of James Roberts," *New Orleans Tribune*, February 21, 2018.

14. Brantley, Michael, "Did the Pirate Jean Lafitte Retire to North Carolina?" historypie.com.

15. Barry, Richard Schiver, "Fort Macon: Its History," *North Carolina Historical Review*, 1950.

16. Watson, Alan D. *A History of New Bern and Craven County*, 122.

17. Miller, Stephen, *Recollections of New Bern 50 Years Ago*, 1873, reprint 1978, 47.

18. Watson, Alan D., *A History of New Bern and Craven County*.

19. Still, William N., Jr., and Richard Stephenson, "Shipbuilding and Boatbuilders in Swansboro 1800–1950," *Tributaries*, October 1995, 10.

Bibliography

"About Swansboro." Town of Swansboro, NC, www.swansboro-nc.org.
Acts and Resolutions of the Second Session of the Provisional Congress of the Confederate States, Held at Montgomery, Ala. Richmond: Enquirer Book and Job Press by Tyler, Wise, Allegre & Smith, 1861. Electronic edition, Documenting the American South, UNC-Chapel Hill, pp. 19–20.
"Address." *Semi-Weekly Standard* (Raleigh), April 21, 1860.
"American Prisoners Watch as British Guards Fire into Their Ranks." National Park Service, https://www.nps.gov/articles/dartmoor-prison.htm. Accessed December 18, 2023.
Angley, Wilson. *An Historical Overview of Beaufort Inlet, Cape Lookout Area of North Carolina.* North Carolina Archives, 1982.
Ashe, S.A. "Captain Ashe Writes of Difference of Taste." *News and Observer* (Raleigh), August 16, 1903.
Barry, Richard Schriver. "Fort Macon: Its History." *North Carolina Historical Review*, vol. 27, no. 2, 1950, pp. 163–177.
"Beaufort, Sept. 3, 1833." *The Newbernian* (New Bern, NC), February 24, 1837.
Beyer, Rick. *The Greatest Stories Never Told.* Harper, 2003.
Bishop, RoAnn. "The Ups and Downs of a Seafaring Man." *Tar Heel Junior Historian*, North Carolina Museum of History, 2008.
Bitzer, G.W., Camera, American Mutoscope and Biograph Company, and Paper Print Collection. *Funeral of Hiram Cronk.* United States: American Mutoscope and Biograph Company, 1905. Video. https://www.loc.gov/item/00694398/.
"Blacks and the Battle of New Orleans: The Story of James Roberts." *New Orleans Tribune*, February 21, 2018.
Blain, Mary F. *Games for Hallow-e'en.* New York, 1912.
Branch, Paul. *Fort Macon.* Nautical & Aviation Publishing Company of America, 1999.
Brantley, Michael. "Did the Pirate Jean Lafitte Retire to North Carolina?" historypie.com.
Brown, J. "United States of America, North-Carolina District. To the Marshal of the District, Greeting." *Newbern Sentinel* (New Bern, NC), September 18, 1819.
[Bryan, John H.]. "Otway Burns and the Snap Dragon." *North Carolina University Magazine*, 2nd. ser. 4 (1855): 407–13, 461–67.
Burke, Kenneth E., Jr. *The History of Portsmouth North Carolina.* University of Richmond, 1958.
Burns, Otway. "Challenge Accepted." *Newbern Sentinel* (New Bern, NC), January 4, 1823.
Burns, Otway. "Communications." *New Bern Sentinel* (New Bern, NC), December 7, 1831.
Burns, Walter F. *Captain Otway Burns: Patriot, Privateer and Legislator.* New York, 1905.

Bibliography

Butler, Lindley S.. "Otway Burns: A Legendary Privateer of the War of 1812." *Tributaries*, October 1998.
Butler, Lindley S.. *Pirates, Privateers and Rebel Raiders*. University of North Carolina Press, 2015.
"Cannon on Pollock Street Not from Snap-Dragon, of Revolutionary Time." *Daily Journal* (New Bern), February 8, 1901.
"Captain Otway Burns." *News and Observer* (Raleigh), July 11, 1901.
Carr, Dawson V. "Lightships." *NCPedia*, 2006.
"Challenge Accepted." *Newbern Sentinel* (Newbern, NC), January 4, 1823.
Chambers, Robert. *Book of Days*. W & R Chambers, 1864.
Chidsey, Donald Barr. *The American Privateers*. Mead, Dodd, 1962.
Coggeshall, George. *History of the American Privateers and Letters of Marque*. Privately printed, 1856.
Daniel, Beverly. "Marshal's Sale." *Fayetteville Weekly Observer* (Fayetteville, NC), June 23, 1825.
Daughan, George C. *1812: The Navy's War*. Basic Books, 2013.
Dean, Jim. "Otway Burns and the *Snap Dragon*." *Wildlife in North Carolina*, Vol. 48, Issue 6, June 1984.
"Died." *Raleigh Register*, June 27, 1823.
"Dinner to Lieut. William A. Eliason." *New Bern Sentinel* (New Bern, NC), September 15, 1827.
"Early June 2–3 Hurricane of 1825." North Carolina Shipwrecks, March 19, 2011, northcarolinashipwrecks.blogspot.com.
Eden, Steven. "Commodore Barney at the Bladensburg Races." *Naval History Magazine*, Vol. 24, No. 5, October 2010.
"Eighth of January." Thesession.org.
"Elizabeth City (NC) Oct. 8." *Raleigh Register*, October 21, 1825.
Encyclopedia of the War of 1812. ABC-CLIO, 1997.
"Engineer Orders." *New Bern Spectator* (New Bern, NC), October 24, 1829.
"Erect Monument to Capt. Otway Burns." *Asheville Citizen*, June 28, 1909.
Ewbank, Anne. "How to Play a Fiery Victorian Christmas Game and Not Get Burned." *Atlas Obscura*, December 16, 2020.
"From the Baltimore American." *Sentinel* (New Bern, NC), April 19, 1828.
Gardiner, Robert, ed. *The Naval War of 1812*. Caxton Editions, 1998.
Gaskill, Matilda. "The *Snap Dragon*." *Beaufort News*, April 28, 1927.
"General Assembly, House of Commons." *Raleigh Register*, January 9, 1829.
Gilje, Paul A. "The End of the War: The Dartmoor Massacre and a Tainted Place." *Commonplace: The Journal of American Life*, Vol. 12, No. 4, July 2012.
Good, Timothy S., ed. *American Privateers of the War of 1812: The Vessels and Their Prizes as Recorded in* Niles' Weekly Register. McFarland, 2012.
Greene, Lucy. "Early History." In Joseph Parson Brown, ed., *The Commonwealth of Onslow*. Owen G. Dunn, 1960.
"Harbor of Beaufort." *Weekly Standard* (Raleigh), December 26, 1834.
"He Named Ship in Honor of Burns." *Beaufort News*, July 3, 1941.
Hickey, Donald R. *The War of 1812: A Forgotten Conflict*. University of Illinois Press, 2012.
Hill, Mrs. Fred, ed. *Historic Carteret County, North Carolina 1663–1975*. Carteret County Historical Society, 1976.
"His Brave Deeds to Be Remembered." *News and Observer* (Raleigh), July 25, 1901.
Howard, Hugh. "Joshua Barney against the British." Historynet.com. Accessed December 15, 2020.

Bibliography

"I'm Thinking." *Rocky Mount Telegram* (Rocky Mount, NC), September 13, 1952.
Jackson, Donald, and Dorothy Twohig, eds. *Diaries of George Washington*, Vol. 6. January 1790–December 1799. University of Virginia Press, 1979.
"Joshua Barney." American Battlefield Trust, battlefields.org. Accessed December 15, 2020.
Lawrence, R.C. "Captain Otway Burns." *The State*, August 30, 1941.
"Laws of N. Carolina Passed in 1827–28." *North Carolina Star*, February 14, 1828.
Lemmon, Sarah McCulloh. *North Carolina and the War of 1812*. North Carolina Division of Archives, 1971.
Lemmon, Sarah McCulloh, and Tucker Reed Littleton. "Otway Burns, Jr." *NCPedia*, 1979.
Lewis, Durward "Dee." Interview, 2020.
Littleton, Tucker R. "A Brief Biographical Sketch of the Life and Exploits of Captain Otway Burns, Jr." https://swansborohistory.blogspot.com/2008/10/otway-burns-shipbuilder-and-privateer.html.
Littleton, Tucker R. "North Carolina's First Steamboat." *The State*, November 1977.
Maclay, Edgar Stanton. "The Exploits of Otway Burns, Privateersman and Statesman." U.S. Naval Institute *Proceedings*, May 1916, www.usni.org.
Maclay, Edgar Stanton. *A History of American Privateers*. D. Appleton, 1899.
"Maritime National Historic Landmarks: Lightships." National Park Service, www.nps.gov.
Meares, Hadley. "The Dramatic Life and Mysterious Death of Theodosia Burr." *Atlas Obscura*, March 9, 2022.
Miller, Stephen. *Recollections of New Bern 50 Years Ago*. 1873, reprint 1978.
Mobley, Joe A., ed. *The Way We Lived in North Carolina*. University of North Carolina Press, 2003.
Moore, Elizabeth. *Records of Craven County, Vol. I*. Genealogical Recorders, 1960.
"Neutrality Proclamation, 22 April 1793." *Founders Online*, National Archives, https://founders.archives.gov/documents/Washington/05-12-02-0371. [Original source: *The Papers of George Washington*, Presidential Series, Vol. 12, *16 January 1793–31 May 1793*, ed. Christine Sternberg Patrick and John C. Pinheiro.]
"Newbern, June 4." *Raleigh Register*, June 14, 1825.
"North Carolina 1814 House of Commons, Newbern Borough." *A New Nation Votes: American Election Returns 1787–1825*. Tufts University. https://elections.lib.tufts.edu/catalog/kp78gh255.
"Notice." *Carolina Federal Republican* (New Bern, NC), October 2, 1813.
"Notice." *Newbern Sentinel* (New Bern, NC), September 12, 1818.
"Notice." *Newbern Sentinel* (New Bern, NC), October 10, 1818.
"Notice." *Newbern Sentinel* (New Bern, NC), February 16, 1822.
"Of Older Date." *Daily Journal* (New Bern, NC), February 8, 1901.
"Otway Burns and the *Snap Dragon*." *North Carolina University Magazine*, UNC-Chapel Hill, 1855.
Otway Burns Papers, July 6, 1809, Onslow County Clerk of Court and Register of Deeds.
"Otway Burns Statue." *News and Observer* (Raleigh), July 8, 1909.
"Overlooking the Sea in Eastern Carolina." *Twin-City Daily Sentinel* (Winston-Salem, NC), December 14, 1921.
Patrick, Christine Sternberg, and John C. Pinheiro, eds. *The Papers of George Washington*, Presidential Series, Vol. 12, *January–May 1793*. Charlottesville: University of Virginia Press, 2005, pp. 472–474.
Paul, Mary, and Grayden Paul. *Folklore, Facts and Fiction about Carteret County in North Carolina Told in Story and Song*. Beaufort Historical Association, 1972.
Phalen, William. *The First War of the United States: The Quasi War with France 1798–1801*. Vij Books India, 2018.

Bibliography

Pool Family Papers, Outer Banks History Center, North Carolina Department of Natural and Cultural Resources.
"Proscription." *Fayetteville Weekly Observer* (Fayetteville, NC), July 16, 1845.
"Public Sale." *Carolina Federal Republican* (New Bern, NC), September 18, 1813.
"Reminiscences of Privateering in the War '12." *The Newbernian* (New Bern, NC), November 14, 1874.
Robinson, Jack. *Otway Burns and His Ship the* Snap Dragon. Lulu, 2006.
"A Scrap of Carolina History." *Goldsboro Messenger* (Goldsboro, NC), July 13, 1874.
"*Snap Dragon* Log Book." *New Bern Weekly Journal* (New Bern, NC), February 27, 1896.
"The *Snap Dragon's* Cannon." *Charlotte News* (Charlotte, NC), February 7, 1901.
Sprunt, James. *Chronicles of the Cape Fear River, 1660–1916.* East Carolina University Digital Collections, pp. 138–139. Accessed December 18, 2023.
"State Legislature." *Weekly Raleigh Register*, December 9, 1834.
Stephenson, Richard A., and William N. Still, Jr., eds. *The Submerged Cultural Resources of Swansboro, North Carolina.* Program in Maritime History and Nautical Archaeology, East Carolina University, May 1994.
Stick, David. "Privateers." *NCPedia*, 2006.
Still, William N., Jr., and Richard Stephenson. "Shipbuilding and Boatbuilders in Swansboro 1800–1950." *Tributaries*, October 1995.
Still, William N., Jr., and Richard Stephenson. *Shipbuilding in North Carolina 1688–1918.* North Carolina Office of Archives and History, 2021.
"A Suggestion for the Fair." R.W. Humphrey, letter to the editor, *Daily Journal* (New Bern, NC), December 14, 1895.
"Summary." *The Harbinger* (Chapel Hill, NC), January 23, 1834.
Swain, David L. "Proclamation, by the Governor of N. Carolina." *Fayetteville Weekly Observer* (Fayetteville, NC), February 19, 1833.
U.S. Census, 1850.
von Graffenreid, Christoph. "Relation of My American Project." *Von Graffenreid's Account of the Founding of New Bern*, c. 1714.
"The War Comes to Portsmouth." National Park Service, www.nps.gov.
Watson, Alan. *Internal Improvements in Antebellum North Carolina.* University of North Carolina Press, 2002.
Watson, Alan D. *A History of New Bern and Craven County.* Tryon Palace Commission, New Bern, 1987.
Watson, Alan D. *Onslow County: A Brief History.* Division of Archives and History, North Carolina Department of Cultural Resources, Raleigh, 1995.
Williams, Wiley J. "Rip Van Winkle State." *NCPedia*, 2006.
Zimmerman, James Fulton. *Impressment of American Seamen.* Columbia University, 1925.

Index

Abernathy, Charles L. 174
Active 73
Adams, John 25, 101
Adams, John Quincy 27, 100
HMS *Adonis* 77–78, 83
Adventure 107
Albemarle Sound 145
Alexandria 117, 143
Algonquian village 15
Almeda, Capt. 93
Alston, John 141, 146
Alston, Theodosia Burr 13, 141–147
Amelia Island 66
America 43
"America" 174
American Revolution 34–35, 38, 48, 101, 139
Anaconda 37, 68
Ann 80–81
Ann Street Methodist Church 174
Anthony, Joseph 89–90, 93
Antonio, Manuel 115
Arawari River (also Arawan) 90
Argo 114
USS *Argus* 36
Armistead, Gen. Lewis 21
Armstrong, John 152
Armstrong, Solomon 152
Arrington, Archibald H. 137
Aruba 58
Ashe, S.A. 135
Asheville 133
Asheville Citizen 160
Atlantic Hotel 105, 160
Atlas 68

Bailey, John "Yellow Jacket" 160
Bald Head Island 146
Baltimore 18, 37, 66, 72, 93, 97–99, 113
Bank of Cape Fear 131

Bank of New Bern 131
Bank of North Carolina 133
"bankers" or "wreckers" 142
Baratarian pirates 103
Barbary states (pirates) 26
Barbary War 26
Barbour, Ruth 47, 156, 164; *The Cruise of the Snap Dragon* 47, 156, 164
Barker, Thomas 89
Barney, Joshua 97–98
Batchelor's Creek 22
Bates, Captain 83
Bath 17, 106
Battle, Kemp 151, 156
Battle, Lott 47
Battle, William H. 125
Battle of Boston Harbor 67
Battle of Lake Erie 69
Battle of Leipzig 69
Battle of Moraviantown 69
Battle of New Orleans 24, 35, 103, 167
Battle of Tippecanoe 30
Battle of the Thames 69
Bayard, James 100–101
Beanes, William 99
Bear Inlet 16
Beaufort 15–18, 32, 38, 47–48, 58, 62–63, 68, 72–73, 75–76, 81, 83–87, 89, 94, 105–107, 110–111, 114–117, 120, 123, 130–131, 133, 135, 137, 139–140, 141, 145, 148, 150, 153, 155–156, 158, 160–164, 167, 169, 172, 174
Beaufort Inlet 111
Beaufort News 162, 172
Bell, Elijah 131–132
Bellingham, John 33
Berlin Decree 30
Bermuda 75–76
Bertie County 132
Bettie 163, 169

191

Index

Biscayne Bay 62
Blackbeard (Edward Teach) 10, 106
Blackman's Creek 22
Bladensburg Races 98
Bligh, William 148
Bogue 15
Bogue Banks 117, 122
Bogue Point 116
Bogue Sound 17, 117
Bogue's Inlet 116–17
Bonnet, Stede 107
Borden, Joseph 133
Borden, Thomas 133
Borden, William H. 128, 130–131
Boston 18, 37, 108, 169
Boston Harbor 72
bounties 30, 64, 66
HMS *Bounty* 148
Brant Island lightship 136–137
brick making 112, 116, 118–122
Bridgeport 114
Brigden, Edward A. 92
British blockade 45, 64, 66
British burning Washington, DC 99
British Guinea 65
Brock, Isaac 65
Broke, Phillip 72
Brown, Aycock 162–163
Brown, James 70–71, 78, 81
Bryan, James W. 135
Bryan, John H. 150–151
Buenos Aires 154
Buncombe County 126, 129
Burdick, Benjamin F. 146
Burke County 129
USS *Burns* 161
Burns, Charles O. 152
Burns, Edwin Oscar 152
Burns, Eugene 152
Burns, Harriet Hall 152
Burns, I.R. 152
Burns, Jane Hall 105–106, 137
Burns, Jane Smith 137, 139
Burns, Jerome 152
Burns, Joanna Grant 17, 22, 84, 96, 105
Burns, Lillian 152
Burns, Martha Armstrong 152
Burns, Owen 84, 96, 105, 137, 149, 152, 171
Burns, Owen, Jr. 152
Burns, Richard 152

Burns, Walter Francis 50, 139–140, 152, 155, 163
Burns, William 92
Burns family 15
Burnsville 36, 123, 132, 147, 156, 160, 172
Burr, Aaron 13, 141, 143
Burr, J.G. 165
Burton, H.C. 117
Butler, Lindley 47, 95, 151
Butler, Trison 89

Cadiz 63, 72
Calhoun, John C. 110
Camp Lejeune 17
Campbell (prisoner) 82–83
Campbell, Marsden 130
Canada 26, 31
Canady, Richard 152
cannonades 38
Cape Antonio 62
Cape Farewell 44, 79
Cape Fear and Yadkin River Railroad Company 131
Cape Fear River 32, 68, 109, 124, 128–129
Cape Florida 62
Cape Francis 79
Cape Henry, VA 29, 75–76
Cape Lookout 72, 93, 106–107, 114, 138
Cape of Good Hope 154
Cape Race 73, 91
Cape San Roque 44
Captain James Seawell and Associates 109
Captain Otway Burns Byway 162
Carolina Federal Republican 81, 159
Carolina Sentinel 112
Caroline 44
carronades 38
Cartagena 59–61
Carteret, George 105
Carteret County 105, 113, 116, 120, 123–124, 128, 130, 132, 136, 147–148, 150–151, 163, 172
Carteret County History Museum 163
Chadwick, James 86–87, 148
Chambers, Robert 156; *Book of Days* 156
Charleston 37
Charlotte 133, 168
Charlotte News 139
Charlotte Observer 153

192

Index

Chase, William M. 160, 163
Chattoka 19
Cherokee County 130
USS *Chesapeake* 36, 67, 72
Chesapeake and the *Leopard* 29
Chesapeake Bay 50, 97, 99
Christian, Fletcher 148
Churchill, Charles 47
Civil War 131, 138, 168
Civilian Conservation Corps 169
Clarendon Steamboat Co. 109
Clark, Isaac. 92
Clark, Walter 36, 147, 151, 156, 158, 160, 174
Clay, Henry 100, 102
Clay, Jonathan 102
Cleopatra 93
Clubfoot and Harlowe Canal Company 117, 125–126, 128–129, 133
Cockburn, Sir George 68, 98
"Columbia, Gem of the Ocean" 174
Comet 43, 83
Confederate States 35, 152, 159–160
USS *Congress* 36
Connecticut 37
USS *Constellation* 36, 171
USS *Constitution* 36, 65
Convention of 1835 132
Convention of Mortefontaine 26
Coon, Samuel 146
Core Banks 106–107
Core Sound 106, 123
Coree Indians 106
Craney Island 16
Craven County 48, 105, 123, 132–133
Cronk, Hiram 166
Cuba 62, 96
Cumming, David A. 146
Curaçao 58
Currituck 17, 66
Currituck Inlet 130
Cuthbert, James 89

Daily Journal of New Bern 139, 143, 147
Daily National Intelligencer 165
Daniel, Marshal Beverly 114
Daniels, Josephus 162–163
D'Aquin, Louis 103
Dartmoor 42, 73, 76, 95, 148, 166–167
Dartmoor Massacre 166
Daves, Graham 143, 147

Davidson County 126
Dean, Jim 35
Decatur, Stephen, Jr. 25, 65, 100
Decatur, Stephen, Sr. 35
Declaration of Paris 1856 35, 159
DeCokely, Benjamin (also D. Coakley or D. Cokely) 50, 78, 89, 95
Deep River 124
DeFarges, Jean 146
Democratic Party 138
Detroit 65
Divorce and Alimony Committee 128
Dixon, Experience Grant 149
Dodge, D.K. 109
HMS *Dominica* 54
Don João Sixto 111
Drake, Sir Francis 35
Dram Tree 110
Drum Inlet 106
Dudley, Edward B. 132
Duke of Beaufort 106
Duke of Wellington 103
Duke University 172
Dunkards 130
Duplin County 130
Dutch Guiana (Suriname) 91

Earl of Granville 105
Edenton 37–38, 47, 68, 132
Eliason, William 117–122
Elizabeth 80, 93
Elizabeth (flat) 112
Elizabeth City, NC 85, 107, 115, 133, 143–145
Ellikson, Captain 114
Engineer Orders 119–120
USS *Enterprise* 36
Equal Rights Party 138
USS *Essex* 36

USS *Falmouth* 152
HMS *Fawn* 57–58
Fayetteville 108, 124, 129, 133
Fayetteville Weekly Observer 114, 137
Federal Republic 63
Federalists 26
Fernando 63
Fernando de Lemos, Truth and Fiction 143
Ferrand, William Pugh 111
Ferrand House 111

Index

Ferrier, Lorenzo 168
Ferrill, Bennett 47
Fillis 58, 63
Fish House Liars 164, 169
Fletcher, Henry 92
Florence, Italy 160
Florida 104, 113
Florida Keys 62
Fort Dobbs 116–117
Fort Fisher 107
Fort Hampton 116–117
Fort Johnson 110
Fort Macon 112, 116–118, 120, 168, 170
Fort McHenry 100
Fort Monroe 117
Fox 43
Fox, Captain 74, 77–78
HMS *Frolic* 65
Frying Pan Shoals 109
Fulton, Robert 108

Gadsby's Tavern 143
Gallatin, Albert 66, 100, 102
Gardner, John 89
HMS *Garland* 53
Gaston, William 31
Gauthier, Thomas N. 109
Gayarre, Charles 143
George, Malea 92
George, Peter 92
Georgetown, SC 142
Georgia 37
German Palatinate 18
Ghent, Belgium 100
Globe 90
Gloucester 172
Glover, Alexander 89
Goldsboro Messenger 153
Good Intent 74
Governor Tompkins 68
Graham, Edward 20
Graham, William 47, 94–95
Grand Bank 72, 76
Grant, Col. Reuben 18
Granville County 105, 132
Graveyard of the Atlantic. 142
Graveyard of the Atlantic 144
Great Dismal Swamp 16, 127
Great Lakes 36, 100
Green, Thomas 92
Green Brothers 15

Greenland 44, 79
Greensboro 133
Gretiot, Charles 119–120
Griffith, Moses 89
HMS *Guerrière* 65
Gulf of Venezuela 56
Guthrie, Bob 163, 167
Guthrie, James 89

Halifax (Canada) 72, 95–96
Halifax County 132–133
Hamilton, Alexander 13, 141
Hamilton, William S. 32
Hammocks Beach State Park 17
Hampton Roads 50
Happy 80
Hare 96
Harker, Ebenezer 15, 169
Harker's Island 16, 150, 169
Harpy 68
Harris, Sandy 132
Harrison, William Henry 27, 30, 65, 68
Hart, George L. 114
Hart, John 92
Hartford Convention of 1814 31, 101
Hartley, Abner 132
Harvey, John 47
Hatteras 138, 143
Havana 62–63
Hawk 37, 94
Hawkins, William 31, 108
Hawood, William H., Jr. 132
Helen, Isaac 124
Henderson, Alexander 133
Henrietta 73, 83
Henrietta (steamship) 108, 110
Henry 122
Hero 37, 171
Hertford 133
HMS *Highflyer* 72
Hillsborough 133
Historical Sketches of North Carolina from 1584–1851 155
Hornady, the Rev. Mr. 174
Horne, Moses 89
USS *Hornet* 35, 65, 67
Hull, Isaac 65
Hull, William 64–65
Humphrey, R.W. 147
Hunter, John L. 138
Hutchinson, George 72

Index

impressment 22, 27–28, 104
In Search of Speed Under Sail 150
Intercoastal Waterway 17
Irresistible 111

Jackson, Andrew 27, 35, 102–103, 124, 130, 136, 138, 167
Jacksonville 17, 140
Jamaica 61, 96
James River 19
Jane 73
HMS *Java* 65
Jay Treaty of 1795 24, 29
Jefferson, Thomas 21, 25–26, 31, 101
USS *John Adams* 36, 152
Johnson, Robert 146
Johnson, William 115
Joiner, Andrew 130
Jones, Cadwallader 130
Jones, John F. 130
Jones, John Paul 13, 35, 44, 165
Jones, William 98
Jones County 105

Kemp, Captain 93
Kemp, Rodney 150, 163, 167, 169–170
Key, Francis Scott 100
King, Asa 111
King, William 31
King's Packet 37

"Lady Blessington" 139
Lafayette 129
Lafitte, Jean 35, 103, 167–168
Lake Mattamuskeet 124
Lake Ontario 36
Lambert, Henry 65
Langdon, Capt W. 50
Latham, Fred P. 132
Lawrence, James 67, 72
Lawson, John 19
lays 40
Leecraft, Benjamin 129, 133
Lennoxville 86
Lenoir County 132
Leopard 114
HMS *Leopard* 95
letters of marque 10, 37–38, 47
Levere 45, 150, 171
Lewis, Durward (Dee) 116, 139, 143, 148–149, 163–164, 167

Lewis Walpole Library at Yale University 145
Library of Congress 101
lightships 136
Lincoln, Abraham 21, 152
Lincolnton 133, 168
Little Belt 30
Littleton, Tucker 165
Lockhardt, William B. 132
Locofoco 137–138
Long Tom 38
Lords Proprietors 106
Louis XVI, King 24
Louisiana 37, 143
Louisiana Purchase 102
Love, Thomas George 154
Lovely Lass 37, 94

HMS *Macedonian* 65
Machapunga Indians 106
Maclay, Edgar Stanton 13, 94, 124, 165
Macon, Nathaniel 116
Macon County 129
Madison, Dolley 99
Madison, James 31, 33, 64–66, 98, 100–101
Mahler, F. 163
Maine 37
Manifest Destiny 104
Manley, Matthew 132
Mann, Polly 144
Manney, Dr. James 117–121, 123, 131–133, 168, 171
Manumission Society 127
Maraca 90
Maracaibo 56
Mariners' Museum 95
Marshall, Thomas 130, 133
Marshallberg 169
HMS *Martin* 95
Martin, Francis X. 7–9, 49–50
Maryland 37
Masons 154, 160
Massachusetts 37
Maysville 149
McCrohon's Creek 22
McFarlane, John 146
McKay, James 130
McKinley, James 47
Mebane, A. 132
Mebane, James 130

Index

Melampus 29
Melville Island 95
Menonists 130
Mercury 68
Merrihaw, Capt. 146
Miller, John 47
Milton 133
Mitchell, William 50
Monroe, James 26–27, 30, 110
Monroe Doctrine 104
Monroe-Pinkney Treaty of 1806 29
Montgomery, George W. 133
Moravians 130
Morehead, John Motley 169
Morehead City 47, 107, 144, 169, 171
Morganton 133
Morning Chronicle 89
Morse, Charles 92
Mosquito Coast 61
Mosquito Fleet 98
Mount Airy 160
Museum of the Albermarle 145
Myers, Joseph 89

Nags Head 142, 144
Nantucket 72
Napoleon I 24, 28, 29, 65, 69, 97, 168
Nash County 137
National Intelligencer 99
USS *Nautilus* 36
Naval Chronicle 89
Neptune 72
HMS *Nettler* 54
Neuse River 7, 19, 48–49, 94, 108, 125, 130
Neutrality Proclamation 24
New Bern 7, 12, 18, 20–21, 32, 37–38, 47–50, 64, 68, 70, 81–83, 94, 106–107, 110–113, 115, 117, 129, 132–133, 164, 171–172
New Bern Naval Reserves 174
New Berne Weekly Journal 159
New Hampshire 37
New Orleans 66, 102–103
New River 16, 32
New Town 15
New York 18–19, 37, 45, 101, 113–114, 117, 141–142, 145–146, 155, 160, 163, 166
New York Advertiser 146
New York Times 146

Newbern Sentinel 110–112, 115, 118, 132, 154, 165, 171
Newbern Spectator 119–120
The Newbernian 84, 95
Newfoundland 44, 72–73, 78
Newport 65
Newport News 95
Newport River 125
Ney, Peter 168
Niles, Hezekiah 42–43
Niles' Weekly Register (also known as *Niles' Register, Weekly Register*) 42–43
Noe, Thomas P. 174
Norcom, Fred 132
Norfolk 48, 50, 70, 85
Norfolk 107
North Carolina Archives 172
North Carolina Farmer 127
North Carolina Gazette 21, 50, 159
North Carolina House of Commons 124, 127–133
North Carolina House of Representatives 163
North Carolina Maritime Museum 172
North Carolina Senate 124, 130, 132–133
North Carolina Supreme Court 127
North Carolina University Magazine 155, 159
North River 105, 110, 169
North Sea 68
Nova Scotia 44, 71, 95

Ocracoke 68, 70, 72, 76, 137, 162
Ocracoke Inlet 93, 138
Odd Fellows Lodge 169
Olcott, Jedediah 45
Old Burying Ground 137, 139, 174
Old Providence 61
Old Topsail 114
Olde Brick Store 111
USS *Oneida* 36
Onslow County 16, 18, 105, 152, 160, 162, 174
Onslow County Court 17
Orders in Council 26, 30, 32–33, 102
Orinoco River 93
Otway 163, 169
Otway Burns Boys 162
Otway Burns Chapter of Sea Scouts 162

Index

Otway Burns Chapter of the Daughters of the American Revolution 162
Overman, Mrs. J.P. 144
Overstocks, William 142
Ownsby, Thomas 132

Pakenham, Edward 103
Pamlico Sound 45, 72, 105, 137
Pamptico District Court 111, 114
Pandora 73
Panic of 1837 123, 136
Paramaribo 91
Parker, Theophilis 47
Pasteur, Dr. Edward 18–22, 31, 45, 47–48, 50–51, 81–82, 112–113
Pasteur, Thomas A. 171
Patriot 142–143, 146–147
Patuxent River 98
Paul, Mrs. Grayden Paul 172; *Unknown Seas* 172
HMS *Peacock* 65
Pearson, Joseph 31
Pennsylvania 37
Pensacola 102
Perceval, Spencer 33
Perry, Oliver Hazard 69
Philadelphia 18–19, 37, 101, 113, 172
Pigott, Ed 172
Pigott, Elijah 48, 107, 133
Pigott, Jaconias 133
Pirates, Privateers, and Rebel Raiders of the Carolina Coast 95
Pitt County 123
Plane 61–62
Pollock, Thomas 106
Ponce 55
Pool, William Gaskins 144
Port Brunswick 107
Port Roanoke 107
Porter, David, Jr. 107
Porter, David, Sr. 35
Portland, ME 17–18, 45
Porto Cabello 59
Portsmouth Island 72, 136–139, 148, 150, 161, 174
Portsmouth (NH) 37
pothouse 61
Potomac River 113
Potter, Van 144–145
POW bounties 41
Pratts 145

President 30, 72
USS *President* 36
Prince-de-Neufchatel 43, 68
Prometheus 108–110, 156, 161, 164–165
Prophet Town 30
Providence 62
Provincetown, MA 66
Provost, George 33
Puerto Rico 55

Quakers 130
Quasi-War 22, 25, 35, 65, 97
Queen Anne's Revenge 107
Queen's Creek 15, 148

Rachael 56
Raleigh 124, 129–130, 132–133, 172
Raleigh 72
Raleigh and Gaston Railroad 135
Raleigh Minerva 165
Raleigh News & Observer 135
Raleigh Register 112, 115, 159
Rambler 111, 154
Randolph-Macon College 116
USS *Ranger* 35
Rattlesnake 68
Reid, James 96
Reminiscences and Memoirs of North Carolina and Eminent North Carolinians 155
Reprisal 80
Revenge 50–52
Richmond Hill 146
Ridgely, Charles G. 47, 171
HMS *Rifleman* 75, 78
HMS *Ringdove* 74
Rip Van Winkle State 3, 127
Roanoke 17
Roanoke Island 147
Robinson, Jack 150
Rockingham 169
Rodgers, John 72
Rogers, William 92
Rossie 98
Rumley, John 137
Russell, Jonathan 32, 100
Rutherford Spectator 132

"The Saga of Otway Burns" 170
St. Croix 54–55
St. John's 74, 77–78

197

Index

St. John's Lodge 20
St. Matthews 52
St. Thomas 52–54
Salem 133
Salisbury 131, 133
Salter Path 169
saltworks 112
HMS *San Domingo* 72
San Jose Indiano 37
Sanders, Charles 47
Sanders, J.W. 147
Santa Maria 111
Santa Marta 58
Saratoga 91
USS *Saratoga* 93
Sarvary, Josephy 103
Savoy Jack 44
Scourge 68
Second Hague Conference 159
Semi-Weekly Standard 132
Seymour, William 89
Shackleford, John 106
Shackleford Banks 106–107, 122
HMS *Shannon* 67, 72
Shawnee 30
Shell Castle 93
Shepard, William 47, 81–82, 171
Shepard's Point 171
Ship Rock (aka Sail Rock Passage) 53
Sierra, Capt. Carinto 81
Signora Ascension 81
Sisters 56
Skidmore, Theodore 84
Skunk 38
slaves 135–136
Smith, James 72–73, 89
Smith, John L. 117–120
Smith's Creek 172
Smithville 109
Smoky Mountain Turnpike 127
Smyrna 137
Snap Dragon 10–13, 47–63, 70, 72–82, 84–87, 89–93, 95–96, 107, 126, 132, 139–140, 145, 148, 150–151, 153, 155–156, 159, 161–162, 164, 166–167, 170–172
Snap dragon (game) 156, 164
Snap Dragon (sailboat) 122
Snap Dragon Chapter of the Daughters of the War of 1812 162
Snow Hill, NC 19

Snyder, John 110
Somerset, Henry 106
HMS *Sophie* 53
South Africa 122
South Carolina 19
South Caroliniana Library 146
Southport 109
Spaight, Gov. Richard Dobbs 20–21, 132
Spanish-American War 168
Spanish Main 52, 55
Sprunt, James 164
Stacy 170
Stanly, John 20–22, 31
Stanly-Spaight duel 171
"Star-Spangled Banner" 100
Stella 149, 170
Stephens, M.C. 133
Stewart, Charles 100
Stick, David 144
Stickney, Theodore 92
Stone, David 31
Straits 116, 172
Styron, W.D. 127
Surinam River 91
Surprize 43
Swain, David L. 126, 133, 154
Swann, Samuel 16
Swannanoa and Laurel River Turnpike Company 130
Swansboro 15, 18, 32, 63, 68, 84, 105, 107–108, 110–111, 141, 161, 165
Swansboro Area Heritage Center 141, 148, 162–163, 165
Swansboro High School 148
Switzerland 18
USS *Syren* 36

Tammany Hall 138
Tarboro 37, 47, 133
Taylor, Carol Wylie 170
Taylor, Isaac 47
Taylor's Creek 111
Tecumseh 30, 65, 69
Tennessee 135
Thamesville 69
Thompson (*Snap Dragon* crew member) 51–52
Thornton, William 99
Tillitt, Mr. 144
Topsail Inlet 106
Tories 48, 83–85

198

Index

Tortola 54
Treaty of Ghent 101
Treaty of Paris 1856 159
Trent River 7, 19, 48, 171
Trinity Bay 80
True-Blooded Yankee 67
Turner, Robert 106
Tuscarora War 19, 106
Twin-City Daily Sentinel 160
Tyrell County 127, 129

USS *United States* 36, 65
U.S. Army Corps of Engineers 117–119, 122
U.S. Coast Guard 136
U.S. Lifesaving Service 138
U.S. Lighthouse Service 136
U.S. Treasury Department 136, 138

Vanderlyn, John 144
Vasquez, Joaquim Jose 111
Venezuela 58, 93
Venus 74
Venus (schooner) 111
USS *Viper* 36
Virgin Islands 52, 54
Virginia 19, 37
von Graffenried, Baron Christoph 18–19

Wadesboro 133
Wake County 132
War of 1812 9, 13, 24, 26–27, 33, 35, 40, 103, 166
War with Tripoli 65, 100
Ward, Enoch 106
Ward's Creek 163, 169

Warrior 113
Washington, George 16, 20, 24, 99
Washington, NC 68, 113, 133
USS *Wasp* 35, 65
Waterman, Thaddeus 37
Weeks, Theophilus 16
Week's Wharf 15
West Indies 18–19, 43–44, 55, 62, 71, 122
West River, MD 46
Wheeler, John Hill 94, 155
Whigs 137–138
White Oak River 15–16, 18, 32, 108, 161
Whitfield, George 132
Wilkesboro 124, 133
Wilkins, Theodora 172
William 56
Williams, Benjamin 21
Willis, J.K. 139, 172
Wilmington 16–17, 38, 43, 48, 68, 107, 109–110, 127–128, 132–133
Wilmington Journal 155
Winder, William H. 98
Winston-Salem 160
World War I 159, 161
World War II 161–162
"wreckers" or "bankers" 142, 144
Wright, John 139
Wyche, James 132

Yadkin County 129
Yancey County 123, 129–131, 160
Yankee 37, 43
yardarm duel 93

Zephyr 45–46, 150, 171

www.ingramcontent.com/pod-product-compliance
Lightning Source LLC
Chambersburg PA
CBHW052100300426
44117CB00013B/2213